You were born with potential.
You were born with goodness and trust.
You were born with ideals and dreams.
You were born with greatness.
You were born with wings.
You are not meant for crawling, so don't.
You have wings. Learn to use them and fly.
Rumi

The Incredible Awesome You!

The Keys to Unlocking Your Bright Future

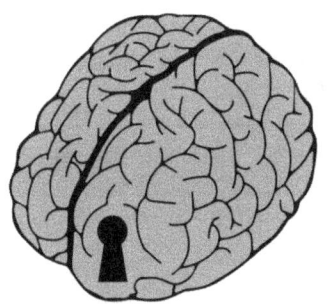

The words you speak become the house you live in!

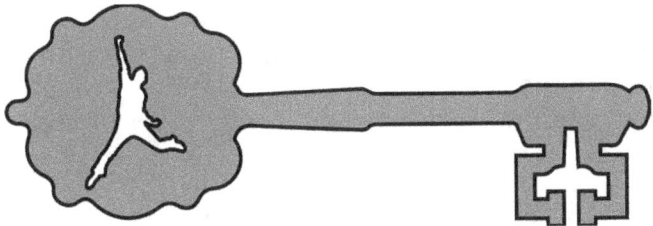

The Incredible Awesome You!: The Keys to Unlocking Your Bright Future © Angelika Jankovic 2019

theincredibleawesomeyou.com

The moral rights of Angelika Jankovic to be identified as the author of this work have been asserted in accordance with the Copyright Act 1968.

First published in Australia 2019 by Gowor International Publishing

ISBN (i.e. 978-0-9923493-0-1)

Any opinions expressed in this work are exclusively those of the author and are not necessarily the views held or endorsed by Gowor International Publishing.

All rights reserved. No part of this publication may be reproduced or transmitted by any means, electronic, photocopying or otherwise, without prior written permission of the author.

Disclaimer
All the information, techniques, skills and concepts contained within this publication are of the nature of general comment only, and are not in any way recommended as individual advice. The intent is to offer a variety of information to provide a wider range of choices now and in the future, recognising that we all have widely diverse circumstances and viewpoints. Should any reader choose to make use of the information herein, this is their decision, and the author and publisher/s do not assume any responsibilities whatsoever under any conditions or circumstances. The author does not take responsibility for the business, financial, personal or other success, results or fulfilment upon the readers' decision to use this information. It is recommended that the reader obtain their own independent advice.

Cover design by: 99 Designs
Key Images by:　José Biotto
Illustrations by: José Biotto & Angelika Jankovic

Your future will be bright, if your attitude is right!

Introduction 10

Prologue: You are the Author of Your Life 13

🗝 Unlocking Your Awesomeness 17

🗝 You Were Born for a Purpose................ 32

🗝 Your Life Is What Your Thoughts Make It.. 43

🗝 Attitude Is Everything 52

🗝 Daily Mental Vitamins 63

🗝 Words for Growth 80

🗝 Goals Are Dreams 87

🗝 Poems, Stories & Words of Wisdom 94

🗝 It's Your Time to Unlock Your Mind..... 115

More About the Author 118

Dedication

I would like to dedicate this book
"The Incredible Awesome You"
to **YOU** the reader!

A Salute for Change!

Every voice that said, 'You can't',
will now be silenced.

Every reason that tells you, 'You will never change', will now disappear.

And the person you were before this moment
no longer exists.

(Adapted from the movie Freedom Writers)

It's your time to unlock your mind!

The Incredible Awesome You!

I think that sometimes we take ourselves for granted. We don't realise how incredibly amazing we truly are.

It doesn't matter what the world, society, or your Facebook feed says about you; we each have a unique gift or special ability in life. You were born for a purpose and your greatest challenge is to discover it and immerse yourself in it. We are each amazing.

Perhaps you sing or draw – I can't do either of those things. Perhaps you have a great engineering mind, or perhaps you have gentleness, kindness and concern for other people at a deeper level than the rest of us. You have unlimited value and inside of you is untapped potential, so let's turn it into active energy!

Create your own path. You will never know what is possible until you attempt the <u>impossible</u>. You will never know what you are capable of until you commit yourself to becoming more. Decide what you want, step forward every day and you will achieve whatever you put your mind to. **Your future is in your hands!**

Well, I never thought I would be an author... and here I am today!

Now is the time...your time. Your future is NOW.

It's time to take responsibility for your life. Decide what your life is all about and live it. Be an original – don't die an imitation.

I will keep telling you that you are important, loving, worthy, creative, inspirational, brave, true, strong, confident, positive, motivated, courageous, determined and most of all enthusiastic, until you finally realise this for yourself!

I encourage you, no, urge you – to wake up to your unique talents and abilities. Don't waste them. You have so much potential to live an amazing life. Can you imagine getting to the end of your life just to discover that you wasted it?

So, let me tell you a vital fact about yourself.

You are truly an Amazing Person!

Introduction

'Write it on your heart that every day is the best day in the year.'
Ralph Waldo Emerson

- ****The Incredible Awesome YOU** is an inspiring and practical book to guide you in understanding that the choices you make today will determine your future success. You can choose to just survive, or you can choose to succeed. But know this – if **YOU** choose to succeed and commit to change, anything is possible! **YOU** owe it to yourself to rise above averageness and self-imposed limitations, to be a passionately authentic and effective human being who 'walks the talk'. **You are unique!** The world awaits the expression of **YOU** in your uniqueness.

- ****The Incredible Awesome YOU** will teach you, that with a little willpower and perseverance, you can change into a positive, motivated person. Develop habits of thinking that will make your life dynamic. People will start to notice a change in you and as a result, will want to spend more time in your company. What a great feeling!

Feeling good about yourself is one of the keys to success.
Success is the result of your determination, rather than your ability. Believe in yourself! It is your own personal inner motivation and desire to do well that will create your success. You were born with greatness, the ability to be the TRUE you, and your best is still ahead of you.

- ****The Incredible Awesome YOU** gives you the insights and tools to implement change. Things do not change. We change. It's about making conscious choices regarding who you are. It's about believing in yourself and knowing that you can achieve whatever you desire. It's about becoming motivated by having a good positive attitude each day. Your future is dictated by the choices you make daily.

- ****The Incredible Awesome YOU** will teach you to think deliberately about your choices. There are so many in life; but which road will you choose to take in order to have great health, wealth and happiness? The quick-fix road? Or the road of planning and setting goals that guide you towards reaching your true potential?

Everyone knows that when you build a house you need, a blueprint to complete the project. If you didn't have a plan, where would you start? A successful life is no different. We need a plan, a blueprint to guide us towards our future happiness.

The real key to life is: If you change your thinking, your surroundings must also change: your attitude, your body, your actions, your home and your whole life. Our thoughts are so close to us that it is difficult, without a little practice, to stand back and look at them objectively. This is something that you can learn, enabling you to take perspective of the way you think. Therefore, you will be able to assess your current situation and put into place building blocks to achieve your desired outcome.

- **The Incredible Awesome YOU** will help you understand how important it is to choose your thoughts wisely. You will learn that you choose your life by the thoughts you entertain. It's not the thoughts that come to you that matter, only the thoughts you choose to think about and dwell on.

Did you know that you can train yourself to choose the focus of your thinking at any given time? It's true. If you are not determined to carefully choose the kind of thoughts you are going to think, it's going to be nearly impossible to shape your life into what you want it to be.

Remember, **YOU** choose your life by the thoughts that you entertain. Training your thoughts is not easy, but it's worth it. I am so passionate about the importance of our thoughts; they are the food that nourishes your mind that determines how successful your life will be.

- **The Incredible Awesome YOU** will help guide you to use the greatest asset you will ever own – your Brain! **Did you know** your brain is the most complex structure in the universe? Within its 1.3 kilograms are one hundred billion neurons to help store away every perception, every sound, every taste, every smell, every action you have ever experienced. Every incident in your life is there waiting only for you to remember. The sooner you realise and accept that your brain and your thoughts create your life and lead you to every success or failure, the better off you will be.

- **The Incredible Awesome YOU** helps you recognise there is no future in the past. Your approach should be from **NO-WHERE** to **NOW-HERE**. **NOW** is the best time to be alive. You don't get another chance at life, so, live life to the fullest.

How to use this book successfully!

Every time you open this book, make sure you have a highlighter ✎, pen ✎ and pencil ✎ so you can mark the pages. When you read a line or paragraph that is meaningful to you, highlight or <u>**underline**</u> it. This simple act alone will increase your retention of that thought or principle, making it easier for you to find it again later. Draw a star ✻ next to any powerful suggestions or something that catches your attention. If you don't agree or understand something, mark it with an exclamation! or a question mark?

I'd be happy to hear your thoughts and feedback via email:
angelika.jankovic@gmail.com

To achieve the best results, read chapter by chapter while making notes directly in the book so you can come back to them, time and time again. They will always offer something new, useful and insightful. You will be able to track your thinking and see whether you have changed over time, which will be quite interesting and a valuable tool for monitoring your growth. It's all up to you! No one else can live your life for you. This is **Your** Challenge...

The Challenge!

Let others lead small lives, but not you.
Let others argue over small things, but not you.
Let others cry over small hurts, but not you.
Let others leave their future in someone else's hands, but not you.

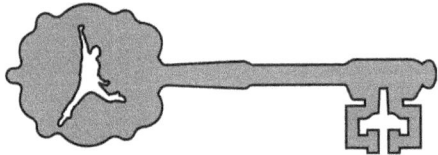

You are the Author of Your Life. My Story.

'The only way to make sense of change is to plunge into it, move with it, and join the dance.'
Alan Watts

Why I wrote... 'You Are the Author of Your Life' in *Superwoman Myths*.

I was approached to write a story about an adversity in my life and how I overcame it. *Superwoman Myths* is a book comprised of stories of women from around the globe sharing their hardships and how they overcame them.

By reading my story, you will soon discover that growing up in a world where you feel lonely and unworthy can have a negative impact on your self-esteem. An adversity in life gives us the strength to keep pushing on. The lessons learnt along the way forms the backbone of who we are today. How you respond and react to situations, no matter how tough, makes you the author of your life.

Destiny is in your hands. Believe, and you will achieve. It is my purpose to help you bust through your own myths so that you too can truly experience life, discover who you are, and really embrace and listen to your heart.

'In the long run, we shape our lives, and we shape ourselves. The process never ends until we die. And the choices we make are ultimately our responsibility.'
Eleanor Roosevelt

I was born in Islington, New South Wales, Australia, into a European family (Serbian father and German mother). Not a good mix. Their fiery temperaments created an explosive environment. They fought like cats and dogs. As the second oldest of five siblings, I always felt I had a duty to assume the role of a leader and protect my siblings from the harsh environment.

We suffered physical abuse and wore bruises throughout most of our childhood. Papa's way of raising children was to beat them. As punishment once, Papa placed some stones on a concrete floor and made me kneel on them for what seemed like eternity.

The physical pain was excruciating. He constantly whipped me and my siblings across our legs and backs with what looked like a solid rubber hose. I'm not sure why, but my mother seemed to turn a blind eye to Papa beating us. Papa was a soldier during World War II, and I think that had a big effect on him. He was high up in the ranks, a captain or something, and I'm sure he had to deal with a lot of traumatic experiences. He never shared any of his past with us. We never even met his family.

It felt as if he was ashamed. Being a soldier was no excuse though, for the harshness that I experienced as a child. Mother and Papa fought frequently. I had this innate need to protect my siblings. I would gather them together and hide in the back garage that was Papa's workshop. It was an amazing experience for me to protect my siblings. I had a great imagination. I was a bit of a storyteller. I would tell them I had a magic wand and make biscuits appear as I would yell, 'Abracadabra!' I was clever and took biscuits from the kitchen, pretended to produce my magic wand, and biscuits would appear from nowhere — much to the surprise of my siblings. They really believed it! My magic wand and stories calmed us all down. Those times were magical for all of us and helped us escape the sounds of our fighting parents.

Born into a European family in the 1950s was not easy going. We were poor and constantly reminded that we were 'wogs'— an abbreviation of 'Western Oriental Gentlemen' used to identify immigrants from Europe. I remember feeling ashamed and different from my peers. It didn't get any easier, from kindergarten to high school. Fellow students were overly rude, insulting and very unkind towards me and my siblings. I recall being in the lunch shed at school, which I dreaded. I would open my lunchbox and the smell of liverwurst or salami sandwiches filled the air. 'What's that smell?' the kids would ask. And I would shut my lunchbox immediately. I just wished my mum would make me jam sandwiches.

My first day of high school was embarrassing. We couldn't even afford a uniform! I felt so humiliated. I liked school, but it was a struggle just keeping up. The language spoken at home was a mix of English and German, thus my English was very limited. I was behind in my studies before classes even started. I had no support at home either. I felt lonely. It took me a long time to master English. It made me feel like I wasn't good enough. All my school reports stated I was an introvert. That had a negative impact on my self-esteem. A sense of unworthiness stayed with me for many years.

One of my dreams was to become a teacher; I knew I was a natural encourager, and I knew what it was like being a child who had to go without and was picked on and ridiculed. I wanted to help others, so they didn't have to feel what I had felt. Unfortunately, the school counsellor shot my dreams to pieces when she said my grades were too low to be a teacher. I was absolutely devastated. In one insignificant moment for the counsellor, my dream to teach, my hopes, and my confidence vanished instantly.

The fighting at home boiled over one too many times, and when I was sixteen years old Mother 'left' Papa. With only three garbage bags full of our possessions, we headed for Sydney by train. The Salvation Army came to our rescue. They provided us with shelter, food and accommodation upon our arrival. My mother, at the age of fifty, took a job as a cleaner at the children's hospital to pay rent and feed us. We lived in a house with twelve rooms, occupied by us and other tenants. The worst part was sharing the one bathroom between all the tenants, but we seemed to make do.

I found myself a job so I could help my mother out financially. My boss gave me a compliment that I will remember forever – 'You have such a beautiful smile when greeting customers.' One of his clients mentioned to him, 'Do you pay your receptionist extra money for that smiling face?' It changed my life—the way in which I viewed myself. I had a renewed sense of confidence and self-respect. This gave me a platform to take ownership of my destiny; it had an amazing impact on my life — a path to realising my goals, aspirations and dreams.

I made up for my school failures by becoming a lifelong learner. The dictionary became my best friend. I attended TAFE to improve my English and undertook various courses, including shorthand and office procedures, to increase my working skills. I took personal development courses to gain self-confidence and be able to speak more confidently. I was on fire with learning!

The turning point in my life came when I was 21 years old. I received a phone call to enter the Miss Australia Quest. I sincerely believed they had the wrong number, so I hung up. They phoned again, and the organisation assured me they wanted to speak with me. It was not a beauty pageant, but instead they were raising money towards The Spastic Centre, now known as the Cerebral Palsy Alliance. When I look back, as I got on stage to thank everyone for all their efforts and contributions towards The Spastic Centre, I realise how this played a major role in increasing my confidence level. It seemed natural at the time to thank people for their incredible support.

My confidence grew over the years, and my dream of becoming a teacher became a reality! I graduated at the age of 47 from the University of Newcastle (NSW) in adult educational studies. My first teaching position was at a private business college, where I taught business studies, communication, and personal development. From there, I developed motivational courses and taught them at evening college. I was awarded Tutor of the Year—the biggest surprise of my life! I'm so glad I kept my vision of becoming a teacher alive, changing many lives along the way.

I later qualified to teach English to foreign students, or TESOL. As soon as I finished the course, my phone rang. I was asked if I would take on a six-month assignment in China. Ever since I was a kid, I had always wanted to go to China — this was after I saw the movie The Inn of the Sixth Happiness starring Ingrid Bergman. Another dream was coming true.

I taught for six months at the China Hong Kong English School in Jiangmen, Guangzhou—a private boarding school for eight hundred students. This experience was incredible. Teaching was so much fun! The students looked upon me as their mum. During my time in China, I felt like a princess. Meals were cooked for me, and cleaners took care of my room. Gone was the childhood poverty I once lived in; it was replaced with a dream life.

Returning to Australia, I enjoyed a newfound confidence and commenced teaching English at local language schools. This has become my real passion. Teaching comes naturally to me, as I knew firsthand how difficult it was for me growing up with a language barrier—just like these students. Today, helping the students push through this barrier and realise their full potential in Australia is the ultimate reward for me.

Destiny is in your hands. Believe, and you will achieve. Overcoming adversity in life gives us the strength to grow. The lessons we learn form the backbone of who we are today. How you respond to situations, no matter how tough, makes you the author of your life.

Remember, everyone has a story... even YOU!

I would like to leave you with my favourite saying that has guided me through the rough times:

Your future will be bright, if your attitude is right.

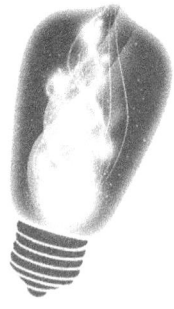

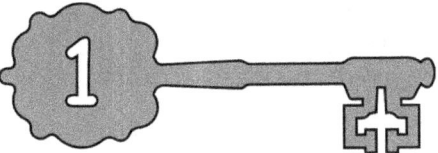

Unlocking Your Awesomeness!

'I would rather die of passion than of boredom.'
Emile Zola

Never Underestimate Your (Hidden) Potential.

You can be whatever you want to be. Inside of you there is all the **potential** to be whatever you want to be – all the energy, to do whatever you want to do. Imagine yourself as you would like to be, doing what you want to do. Once you have this image, take a step each day towards your dream. Just take one step at a time. At times it may seem too difficult to continue, but hold on to your dream. Start to feel and imagine as if the dream has already happened. One morning you will wake to find that you are the person you dreamed of – doing what you want to do, simply because you had the courage to believe in your **potential** and hold on to your dream.

What is potential anyway? Potential simply means 'capable of coming into being or progressing into action.' We all have hidden potential, although most people's potential remains dormant. Questioning yourself about your likes, talents and passion is a way to discover your hidden potential. Action is the next step in moving towards the best of you.

Hidden potential means coming out of your shell and letting the best part of yourself flow out. That's right. *Let the best part of yourself flow out!* Think of all that untapped potential inside each of us. We need to appreciate that we each have a tremendous amount of potential with enormous opportunities waiting for us, if only we looked within ourselves. If you don't believe in yourself, how can you expect others to believe in you? So never underestimate your own unique abilities.

No two people are the same. For example no two plums, oranges, or even apples will ever taste the same. In the same way, the best of one person is not any better than the best of anyone else. I am different from everyone else, therefore I have to express myself in my own way, and not try to copy others. Just the same, you have to respect others and accept the way they express themselves, which may not happen to be your way. This is very important, because no two people are exactly the same, and each and every one of us must express ourselves according to who we are.

Some people are not able to express themselves in the way they should. Most only copy or imitate what others say or do, like an echo that reproduces sound, or a mirror that reflects an image of whatever is placed in front of it. **True self-expression is creation, not imitation.**

What do I mean by this statement? Remember, you are unique in all ways, so whatever you express is the beginning of creating something new rather than simply taking on other people's ideas as your own. By following the crowd, you do not take responsbility for your own uniqueness. *Remember, you have great potential within you, potential that is virtually limitless.* You can create the life that you desire as you are in charge of the incredible awesome you.

Our extraordinary **potential** as human beings is only wasted when it is not used. The greatest waste is to **not** use our minds to excel in life. So, let's understand how our conscious and subconscious minds work together to allow us to grow, develop and create our life.

(Adapted from Mind Power and Your Alpha Rhythm, Peter H. Heibloem)

Conscious Mind – our conscious mind is our 'awareness'; it is our communication centre. It thinks, reasons, calculates, plans, directs all actions of the body, determines results and makes decisions. It is creative, it registers pain, fear, happiness and it sets goals (both long-term and very short-term goals). **The conscious mind makes choices almost every minute of our lives.** For the conscious mind to be able to do these things, it must have a place to pull information from – a storage area; the **Subconscious Mind.**

Subconscious Mind – is our data storage bank. When our conscious mind asks, our subconscious mind gives. The subconscious mind takes in everything we learn and experience in our lifetime. It begins at birth, soaking up information like a sponge, accumulating data as we grow and experience life. It also begins forming beliefs based on what we learn and what we experience, which determines how we react to everything in our life.

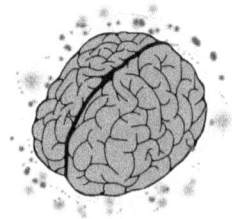

Take a moment to reread the **conscious and subconscious minds** in order to understand how important it is for you to be aware of your thoughts. Know that you can reprogram your subconscious mind so that it goes on its familiar path on autopilot with images you have created for yourself. Try talking to your subconscious mind; tell it that you are limitless, and that you believe all things are possible. Fill it with images of you being all that you dare to dream. *Just checking:* did you take a moment to reread the **conscious and subconscious minds** to understand how important it is for you to be aware of your thoughts?

Hopefully this information will inspire you to take time out and really think about the difference between the **conscious and subconscious minds** to help you towards reaching your true potential.

In summary:

Conscious Mind = awareness, it's our communication centre, whereas **Subconscious Mind** = storage area, it's our data storage bank.

Remember that the subconscious mind does not make choices; it accepts everything, good and bad, positive and negative. The sooner we realise and accept that our brain, mind and thoughts create our life and lead us to every success or failure, the better off we will be. Our extraordinary potential as human beings is only wasted when it is not utilised.

Our conscious and subconscious mind work together to allow us to grow, develop and create our life.

Here is an interesting fact about how our thoughts are affected by our brain.

- Did you know that your brain **cannot** tell the difference between a vividly imagined experience and reality?

Think about when you wake up from a nightmare. You wake up terrified with lots of physical reactions like sweating, breathlessness, tension etc. Yet no physical event has occurred. It all happened in your head; ***your mind did it all***.

The above shows that our subconscious mind does NOT know the difference between fantasy and reality. The mental movie playing in your mind while in a deep sleep seemed so real that your body reacted to it as if it were so. *This can be a very useful tool that you can take advantage of*. Your **inner mental picture** is the most powerful force within you. This is the only reason visualisation works. Whatever the mind keeps thinking of repeatedly, the body will accomplish.

'Whatever the mind can conceive and believe it can achieve.'
Napoleon Hill

This quote gave me insights into my own 'hidden potential' of being an encourager, as I started to believe it and then I achieved it. I LOVE WHO I AM NOW! I followed my dream to become a teacher, with the intention of inspiring people to believe in themselves, to start tapping into their hidden potential, and become aware of the power of purpose in their life, therefore becoming the *captain of their own life.*

Armed with this new knowledge, you can go forward in life with confidence, awareness and understanding, improving virtually every area of your life. You will become more like the person you would like to be, the person who makes incredible things happen in life. The value of your life is brought about by the value of your thinking – think about that. WAY TO GO!

Life is very short, and every day is precious. Capturing the full enjoyment from each day and the thrill of being in charge of your circumstances is one reward for learning to use your brain and thoughts every day in your life. Can anyone afford to be less than their potential? The price is too high! Dedication is needed to get there.

A great example is 'The Slight Edge Philosophy' adapted from Jeff Olson. When you were a tiny, little child, you made your way around the world on your hands and knees crawling. Everyone around you was walking and one day you got it into your head to give that a try. So, little by little, you worked on developing the skills you needed to walk.

You grabbed on to something above you and pulled yourself upright. You stood up, holding on to a table or chair or a big stuffed animal. Wobbly and unsure, you let go, fell down, and tried again and again, until you stood up all by yourself. Then, you took a step.

After days of side-stepping around the coffee table, awkwardly bringing one little foot out from behind the other while you held on to Mum or Dads' fingers, you eventually took your first couple of steps... all alone...all by yourself...and hopefully to the cheers and applause of your family. Baby steps. One at a time. And you were WALKING!

In the process of learning to walk, you probably spent more time failing than you did succeeding. But did you ever have the thought of quitting? Did you ever tell yourself, 'I'm not cut out for walking - guess I'll crawl for the rest of my life?' No, of course you didn't. And that's what being successful is about. How come so many people don't do what they did when they were one or two years old? The answer is alarming, yet simple.

Somewhere along the way in their life, they became unwilling to take baby steps. They lost faith in the universal truth that the simple little disciplines, done again and again over time, would create their success. They forgot about the most proven, powerful success philosophy on Earth — 'The Slight Edge.'

Winning is always a matter of 'The Slight Edge'. If you were to improve by just .003% each day...that's less than half a percent, only a very slight edge...and you kept that up for the next five years, here's what would happen to you.

The first year you would improve 100%. You would be twice what you are today in just one year!

The second year you would improve 200%.

The third year 400%.

And by the end of year five, by simply improving .003% each day you will have magnified your value, your skills and the results you achieve by 1,600%.

That's 32 times more than what you are today!

Just .003% each day...and that's not compounded. That's just adding less than half a percent each day. That's the awesome power of 'The Slight Edge'. It is always operating. It never stops. It's either working FOR you or AGAINST you. It's up to you...it's your choice. Only you can make this become your reality.

'The Slight Edge' Philosophy is based on doing things that are easy; little disciplines that when done consistently over time, add up to big accomplishments. The problem is that all those little things that are easy to do, are just as easy NOT to do. *If it's just as easy not to do something, then why should you take the time and make the effort to do something little each day?* Let's take for instance daily exercise.

There have been countless studies showing that people who don't exercise regularly are more stressed and less happy. The body was made to move. Often you hear people use the excuse that they don't have time. I say make the time and start with baby steps.

Just by starting to exercise for ten minutes a day, taking baby steps, what happens is that you start to form a new habit. Then, increase your exercise weekly by repeatedly using baby steps. Without realising it you are putting into practice 'The Slight Edge' Philosophy. It's gradual but it's achievable, right? By accomplishing this little daily exercise, you have already achieved your .003% improvement. How exciting!

Now let's put 'The Slight Edge' into alignment with your passion. Whatever it is that you desire and dream, start taking baby steps towards making it happen. If you want to be a writer, start writing one paragraph a day. If you want to be a musician, start practicing 10 minutes a day. **Your passion is the key to your success in life**.

Can this be scary? You bet! Especially if everyone around you is saying that you can't do it, it won't work, you're being crazy, etc. Listen to your inner passion and ignore all the naysayers.

By simply putting into practice 'The Slight Edge' attitude and teaching yourself to take baby steps you will be amazed at what you can achieve. Once again, I encourage you to wake up to your unique talents and abilities and don't waste them. You have so much potential to live an amazing life. By using this principle, you may even influence the people around you – imagine that!

While these ideals are important or valuable we need to be realistic.

Balance Is The Key

Everyone has their down moments and periods of struggle. Operating at 100% capacity for 100% of the time is unrealistic. Keep in mind that not every day is going to be easy and perfect, but going the extra mile will make all the difference.

As you continue to read through this book always remember how 'Incredibly Amazing You Truly Are'. So, be all that you can be. The greatest tragedy in life is that millions of people come into this world and leave this world never realising their full potential. Let me emphasis this once more, that millions of people come into this world and leave this world never realising their full potential. Please do not be one of them. You are far more worthy than you may realise.

Every person is in essence two people; the person they are today and that more dynamic, more fulfilled person they could become tomorrow!

Acknowledge that you can be whatever you want to be. There is inside of you all the potential to be whatever you want to be. All the energy to do whatever you want to do. Imagine yourself as you would like to be, doing what you want to do, and each day take a step towards this dream. At times it may seem too difficult to continue, but hold on to your dream. One morning, you will awake to find that you are the person you dreamed of, doing what you wanted to do, simply because you had the courage to believe in your potential and to hold on to your dream.

It's easy to do and it's easier not to do!

🎵**Let's get started towards making a real difference in your life by taking baby steps towards change and thinking through the following questions.**

Right here, right now is the perfect time to be the captain of your life and start on your journey towards creating and reaching your true potential. Start to take baby steps every day. Consider the following question when you are writing down your thoughts. **In everything you do, ask yourself, 'Where is this taking me?'**

Start writing down some ideas and explore the possibility of trying something different. Anything! No matter how crazy they might seem. Just do it! It's a start towards expanding yourself. Then take action and give it a go. Good Luck and have fun along the way.

For example: Would you like to meet someone new? Would you like to learn a new skill? Or, is there something you have been wanting to try? Give it a go...

_____
_____
_____
_____
_____
_____
_____
_____
_____
_____
_____
_____
_____
_____
_____
_____
_____
_____
_____
_____
_____
_____ Dated: __/__/__

🎵 **What do you think is the key that unlocks 'The Slight Edge'? I'll give you a hint. The key is belief and consistency. Belief in yourself and daily action. One of the ways you can build belief is by gaining knowledge. So, what can you do every day to improve your knowledge?**

💡 **Some ideas could be:**
- **Read just 20 pages of an encouraging book every day.**
  Read a book by someone who inspires you, someone you look up to. I started reading 'Think and Grow Rich' by Napoleon Hill. It took him 25 years to write, interviewing the richest and most successful people in the world and then revealing their secrets to success. This book inspired me towards my dreams. What inspires you?

- **Listen to motivational stories –** these will certainly get you fired up and inspired towards creating a better YOU. Are there any audio books, TED Talks, podcasts that encourage you?

_____
_____
_____
_____
_____
_____
_____
_____
_____
_____
_____
_____
_____
_____
_____
_____
_____
_____ Dated: __/__/__

♪**Ask yourself the following key questions. These questions might be hard to answer, but are part of the journey to really discovering yourself. Think of your values — the beliefs and principles that will guide you to your ultimate destiny. There is unbelievable power in living your values. Living your values can give you:**

- **a sense of certainty**
- **an inner peace**

Where would I like to be / What would I like to be doing in three years' time?

___
___
___
___
___

Why do I want to be there / Why do I want to be doing that?

___
___
___
___
___

What is it that I really want out of life e.g. success, happiness?

___
___
___
___
___

Why do I want it?

___
___
___
___
___

What is something I can do on a daily basis to improve myself? If you were made manager of yourself, what three things would you try and improve?

_____
_____
_____
_____
_____
_____

What is one thing that I can achieve within one year that will show me I am working towards my true potential?

_____
_____
_____
_____
_____

Who am I? Please take a moment to describe yourself and evaluate yourself. For example; Are you a leader? Is there something meaningful that you would like to do with your life? Do you like working with others or working alone? What is one of your strengths that could be used to help others?

_____
_____
_____
_____
_____
_____
_____
_____
_____
_____ Dated: __/__/__

Congratulations!

I know the above questions were not easy to answer but you are on the way to discovering the true **YOU**.

The difference between who you are and who you want to be is what you do.

Remember, you are the product of all your thoughts and actions.

It's the key to unlocking your bright future!

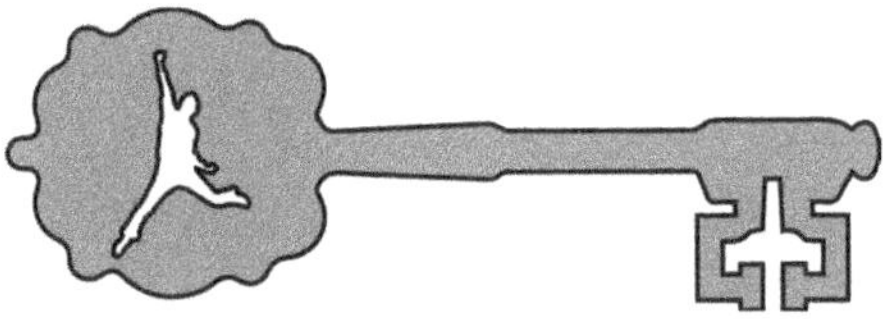

'Nothing will happen to change your life until you consciously step in and start to work with the subconscious mind, otherwise, you will continue in the same pattern you have built up.'

Mildred Mann

♪Now that you have managed to answer the hard questions, it's time to have some fun. Let's do something exciting – let's make a Mind Movie, using the screen of your mind. Remember, your subconscious mind does NOT know the difference between fantasy and reality. Create a Mind Movie of something you want to achieve, visualising it as real as possible. Anything at all that you can imagine. Remember, visualisation puts you there.

Make a plan of your Mind Movie by writing it down first. Start by using your senses. What will you smell, taste, feel, hear and see by visualising your goal? Energise your movie by using emotion and humour to fully enjoy the experience. Get involved and excited about your movie.

For example, imagine you want to be a famous tennis player. Place yourself there. What are you wearing? Who are you playing with/against? Where are you playing? How many people are watching you? What rank are you in the world? Have you signed autographs? Can you see yourself on the front page of a newspaper?

Put all of this into your Mind Movie. Feel yourself serving the ball, the power you have and the crowd cheering you on.

Remember - 'Whatever the mind can conceive and believe it can achieve.' Napoleon Hill

See the change. Make the change. Let's get excited...
It's the beginning of the **NEW YOU!**

In summary:

- Your inner mental picture is the most powerful force within you.
- Whatever the mind conceives, the body will achieve.
- It often helps to mentally experience doing a task successfully first, before you physically act it out.
- Your Mind Movie is a tool that can be used at any time to help you move towards your goals.

Our conscious and subconscious mind work together to allow us to grow, develop and create our life.

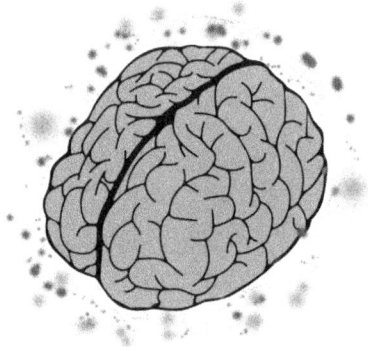

♪**Start to write 'Your Mind Movie Action Plan.'** To get the best results spend a few minutes each day reliving your Mind Movie at all levels, including what you smell, taste, feel, hear and see. Remember to use your imagination to create the exact end result of your goal by using your senses and emotions.

_____
_____
_____
_____
_____
_____
_____
_____
_____
_____
_____
_____
_____
_____
_____
_____
_____
_____
_____
_____
_____
_____
_____
_____
_____
_____
_____
_____
_____
_____
_____ Dated: __/__/__

WAIT – Don't skip this section. It's important to write down your thoughts as this is the first doorway into The Incredible Awesome YOU!

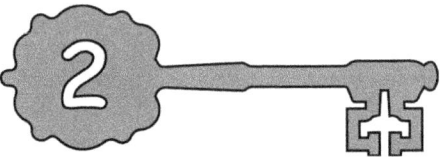

You Were Born for a Purpose!

'Do something today your future self will thank you for.'
Unknown

Now let me introduce you to the most important person in the whole wide world. That person is YOU! You were born to make a difference no matter how big or little. **You are unique!** You are one of a kind, there is nobody like you. Sure, you may have features and characteristics from your family, but as a whole self, there is nobody like you. You were born for a purpose and your greatest challenge is to discover it and immerse yourself in it.

Did you know that the majority of people are going around in circles like a gold fish in a bowl, without achieving anything? It is virtually impossible for anyone to succeed at any level in life without knowing their true purpose, the reason they are here. To be successful you must understand where you are going, why you are going there, and be determined to get there.

Having a purpose inspires confidence and integrity in one's character and attracts the attention of other people. The people who know where they are going and are determined to get there will always find people who are willing to help them succeed. What about YOU? Do you have confidence and integrity?

The only way you are ever going to grow is to do what you have never done before. There is nothing in the universe that you cannot do or be if you are mentally ready. Whenever you are ready, you will find that everything else is ready too. Step outside your daily routine and you will find yourself in an environment you have never been in before – outside of your comfort zone.

Most of us undervalue what we are capable of and we never find out who we are, until life puts us into one of those challenging places, where we must make a choice: to move ahead to the unknown with absolute certainty and commitment, *or* to give up. The unknown is your friend, because that's where the growth is. Step outside your daily routine and chase your dreams. Realise that if you have a dream, your dream needs to be reached and you are the one to make it happen.

That dream will only be brought into reality if you can continually focus on the solutions and not the problems. Things get turned around when you seek solutions and stop focusing on problems. Focus on the value you can add, versus all the fear and challenges that surround you.

We have all heard the old saying, 'The only thing to fear is fear itself.' This is true, but in some ways a better saying might be, 'The only thing to fear is ourselves.' Why? We're all afraid. We're scared of what might or might not happen. We're scared of what we can't change. We're scared of what we won't be able to achieve. We're scared of how others might perceive us.

Fear makes us hesitate. We spend time waiting for the right moment. Then we decide we need to think a little longer. Perhaps we do some research or explore more alternatives. Then before we realise it, days, weeks, months and even years have passed us by. Unfortunately, so have our dreams.

Don't let your fears hold you back. Whatever you've been planning, whatever you've imagined, whatever you've dreamed of, get started on it today. If you want to start a project, take the first step. If you want to change the direction your life is headed towards, take the first step. If you want to study and expand your horizons, take the first step.

What most people don't understand is that passion/purpose is the result of action, not the cause of it. Successful people put their worries aside and get started. They do something. They do anything! Successful people are often afraid, but they're most afraid of looking back and thinking, *if only I had*.

Please don't look back and think, *if only I had*. There is a price that goes with circling around the fish bowl, and the price is giving up your dreams. Those who accept to follow 'the fish' are those who accept 'the norm'. They suffer at the deepest level, the pain of never reaching their true purpose and settling for an average existence. Have a dream and make it real - don't follow the crowd.

Those who go against the crowd are often the people we see as geniuses: Thomas Edison, Christopher Columbus, Steve Jobs, Mother Teresa, even Colonel Sanders. These people went against what others believed they could achieve but succeeded by believing in themselves and following their dreams.

> *When Muhammad Ali was a young and new fighter, he kept repeating the affirmation,* **'I am the greatest'***- several times a day – seven days a week. Most people who followed the boxing world at that time said the opposite. They called him a bum, a jerk, an amateur, a big mouth — in fact, everything but the greatest. Years later, however, even long after he retired, they all call him The Greatest Boxer of All Time.*
>
> *Muhammad Ali said,* **'I am the greatest'** *and* <u>*kept putting this image on the screen of his mind until he believed it and eventually achieved it.*</u>

The only way to change the worth of your life is to be willing to put yourself out there and do something different. Surround yourself with people who produce results and not excuses. Understand the awesome power of persistence and the awesome ingredient of self-belief. Do not give up.

Your life, your choice. Now is the time to take responsibility of your own life. Decide what your life is all about and live it accordingly. Create your own path. You will never know what is possible until you attempt the <u>impossible</u>. You will never know what you are capable of until you <u>commit yourself to becoming more</u>.

Life with a Purpose. Once you work out your purpose and start concentrating your thoughts around it, your brain starts to go into overdrive. When something is important and significant to your life, you then start noticing it everywhere. A classic example is when you purchase a car or a new outfit - suddenly you seem to see it everywhere. What's happened? Those cars and outfits were always there, but your brain is letting you know that this is significant now. Whenever that information is nearby, your brain becomes consciously aware of it. So ultimately with a purpose in mind, things begin to take shape, as your brain is now alert to your thoughts, driving you towards your life's purpose. *The brain, interesting, isn't it?*

If you have a dream, go for it!

Life is an adventure.

So, what's YOUR purpose in life? Ask yourself. What am I here for? What am I doing with my life and where am I going with it? What are my aims? What is my focus? What can I do with my time that is important to me? **The challenge is life itself**. You will be the same person in five years except for two things: the people you meet and the books you read. That's right!

Millions of people before us have learnt many lessons and have recorded them in books for us to dip into their experiences. Allow yourself the gift of reading a minimum of thirty minutes a day. Perhaps miss a TV show or a night out, but don't miss your reading. **LEADERS are READERS**. Reading autobiographies and biographies will give you the tools and insights into how leaders achieve their purpose.

Everyone has a purpose in life, although very few people know what their purpose is. Later in this chapter, I will be asking you to formulate a purpose statement. Let's start thinking about this now. A purpose statement can be summed up in just a few words. It usually begins with "**I AM**..." It's a simple but powerful statement about why you are here and what you are here to do.

Think about your passion. What are you passionate about? Passion means 'a strong enthusiasm or desire.' Passion for your life. Passion for your future career. Passion for your health. Passion for everything you aim to achieve. Passion leads to action, results and finally victory. It's the one ingredient that will push you to new heights every time.

Remember, a person with a passion/purpose in mind, will focus their attention on the information that is available to them to get them to the next step. People who do well in life are rare individuals who don't just believe all the information that is given to them, but instead, they chase quality information that will nourish their lives.

Always read or study the best information you can. *How do you do that?* **The whole key is to know what your purpose is and what you are chasing**. Information is worthless without a purpose. If you know why the information is beneficial to you, then suddenly little things, little ideas and little distinctions that didn't seem to matter, will now make sense. **One simple idea could change your life!**

Philosopher Howard Thurman said, '*Don't ask yourself what the world needs; ask yourself what makes you come alive. And then go and do that. Because what the world needs are people who have come alive.*'

If you know your purpose, go to people who are currently producing results. They may be interested in guiding you. Use them as a MENTOR or ROLE MODEL. Information shared with you by those who have succeeded, is the nourishment that your mind, emotions and soul cry out for.

Keep a daily journal; it is one of the most powerful ways of refining your information and thoughts. You will begin to feel bulletproof against the daily invasion of limiting thoughts and general beliefs that kill most people's dreams.

LIFE'S FUNDAMENTALS

Know what you want
Know why you want it
Discover your talents
Use them daily
Work Hard, Work Smart
Give Unconditionally
Love Unconditionally
Find Your Purpose
Live Your Purpose!

Even the 'Big Book' talks about PURPOSE in the book of Ecclesiastes 3:1-8, King James Version

*'To every thing there is a season,
and a time to every purpose under the heaven.*

*A time to be born, and a time to die; a time to plant,
and a time to pluck up that which is planted;*

*A time to kill, and a time to heal; a time to break down,
and a time to build up;*

*A time to weep, and a time to laugh; a time to mourn,
and a time to dance;*

*A time to cast away stones, and a time to gather stones together;
a time to embrace, and a time to refrain from embracing;*

*A time to get, and a time to lose; a time to keep,
and a time to cast away;*

*A time to rend, and a time to sew; a time to keep silent,
and a time to speak;*

*A time to love, and a time to hate;
a time of war, and a time of peace.'*

(Did you know that the band 'The Byrd's' even thought that these words were worth putting to music and it became a #1 hit in the 60's?)

**'There's much you can't change,
but there's something important you can change: You.'**
Pastor Rick Warren

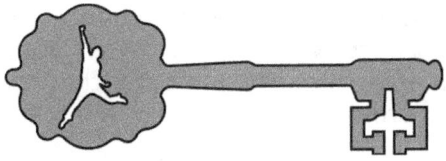

Staying on Target *(Adapted from Hip to Toe Newsletter by Matt Maguire)*

Do you know what percentage of the time Apollo II was on course to the moon in 1969? The answer may surprise you; it was only 3%! In other words, Apollo II was off target for 97% of the time. So how did it manage to make it to the moon if they were off course 97% of the time? The answer comes down to the time they spent constantly correcting and adjusting their course.

If you think about it; it's not that dissimilar to when you are driving your car. You cannot drive in a straight line to reach your destination. There are buildings and shopping malls to navigate around. Unless you are driving a tank, I recommend you follow the road.

In life, we are always checking and adjusting ourselves from simple things like our diet, to the clothes we wear, to which movie star is now the hunkiest! Life is about constant change. The human body is no different. We are constantly evolving and changing. The cells in your body are turning over every second of every day. In the time, it has taken you to read 'Staying on Target' your heart has beat 60 times delivering fresh oxygenated blood to the tissues and removing the waste products from those tissues.

Think about how fantastic that is. You are constantly evolving and changing. But what happens if you are pointing in the wrong direction and no one helps you find the right direction to get you back on course? In time, you'll be further off target.

Can you imagine if no one had spent time correcting the Apollo II, it would never have made it to the moon? Instead, with constant correction and guidance, Apollo II made it to the moon, even though it was pointing in the wrong direction most of the time.

So maybe you might get off target from time to time. That's okay, because with constant correction and guidance and by keeping focused on your purpose, you can reach your potential by looking at problems as stepping stones. One thing that can assist you in achieving this is to create a Statement of Purpose. Let's begin.

🎵 Let's get started towards creating 'YOUR Purpose.'

I say, get up early, yes early, and read something inspirational. Have you noticed when you hear a tune first thing in the morning you seem to hum it for the rest of the day? Put something positive into the brain towards thinking of 'Your Purpose.'

Jump start your day, by jotting down something inspirational with 'your purpose in mind.'

This is important. Start to create your **Statement of Purpose** – what you want, want to do, be, see, have or give. Be specific. The very act of thinking as you write will create a permanent impression in your memory. You will crystallise your thinking.

Now write 'Your Purpose' Statement. Choose your words carefully and be specific. To reinforce your purpose, embrace **Your Purpose Statement** every day by writing it down, printing it and repeating to yourself, especially when you are feeling down. It will have the power to bring you back to your heart, back to that place where your dreams begin. For example:

Walt Disney – Our purpose is to make people happy.

_____
_____
_____
_____
_____
_____
_____
_____
_____
_____
_____
_____
_____
_____
_____
_____ Dated: __/__/__

Find your passion. Live your passion.

🔎 What do you want, what do you want to do, to be, to see, to have or to give? Is there something you want to do, something you think about doing, something you get excited about, yet you don't do it? Be brave and just start doing it. What's stopping you? Make a difference and go the extra mile.

'*If it is to be, it is up to me.*' William H. Johnsen

Take action, action and action! You will start to feel different, you will start to get excited and that feeling of making a difference is ultimately what's most important for your own happiness. Become enthusiastic!

Now start writing your list. What do you want?

_____
_____
_____
_____
_____
_____
_____
_____
_____
_____
_____
_____
_____
_____
_____
_____
_____
_____
_____
_____
_____
_____ Dated: __/__/__

'He who wants to do something finds a way, he who wants to do nothing finds an excuse.'

Arabic Proverb

🔔**This could be challenging,** I know, but what the heck, **JUST DO IT!**

Get up and go for a walk. See the world wake up and be thankful for a beautiful day. Listen to the birds awakening. Do not take your phone or any form of music. Listen to the world going on around you. Then while you are having a great time enjoying the morning, you'll be exercising at the same time.

Did you see anything interesting on your walk? Meet anyone on the way?

Did you have an intuitive feeling towards your purpose? What is your intuition telling you about your current path? One piece of advice I'd like to suggest is never underestimate your intuition. Your inner voice has powerful things to say, especially when you take the time to listen. Here's one of my favourite quotes by Albert Einstein:

'The intuitive mind is a sacred gift, and the rational mind is a faithful servant. We have created a society that honours the servant and has forgotten the gift.'

Did you have an intuitive feeling towards your purpose?

_____
_____
_____
_____
_____
_____
_____
_____
_____

See anything interesting on your walk? Meet anyone interesting?

_____
_____
_____
_____
_____
_____
_____
_____
_____

🔑 **A different way to start on the road to YOUR PURPOSE and make a difference is to start with a pledge (if that works for you). It's a start.**

My Pledge

I pledge to 'show up' in my life as myself,
not as an imitation of anyone else.

I pledge to avoid using the word 'just' to describe myself.
For example, I won't say, 'I'm just a teacher', 'I'm just a student',
or 'I'm just an ordinary person.'

I pledge to give myself 10 minutes of silence and stillness every day to get in touch with my thinking and hear my own voice.

I pledge to use my voice to connect my dreams to my actions.

I pledge to use my voice to empower myself and others.

I pledge to serve my community at least once a year in a way that will benefit other people.

I pledge to ask myself, 'Who am I? What do I believe in? What am I grateful for? What do I want my life to stand for?'

I pledge to sit down and write my own statement of purpose.

I pledge to live my own legacy.

And I pledge to pass it on.

**You can do it. Just believe in Yourself.
You are truly an Amazing Person!**

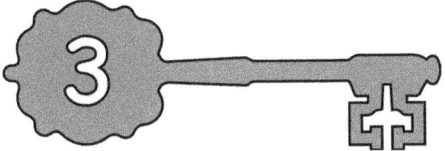

Your Life Is What Your Thoughts Make It!

'Life is a journey, not a destination.'
Ralph Waldo Emerson

The following is by Dr. Ihaleakala Hew Len on **'Thoughts'** which I found very powerful and thought provoking.

'The purpose of life is to be restored back to love, moment to moment.

To fulfil this purpose, the individual must acknowledge that he is 100% responsible for creating his life the way it is.

He must come to see that it is his thoughts that create his life the way it is moment to moment.

The problems are not people, places, and situations, but rather the thoughts of them.

He must come to appreciate that there is no such thing as "out there".'

(Read it again and let the words sink in!)

Our thoughts make us who we are. Thoughts rule the world. If you really understand it, thoughts have ruled the world from the beginning. All the cities in any country started as a thought, or an idea in someone's mind. Every invention, cure, school, business and so on - the list is endless. Thoughts created all that. It started in someone's mind.

YOUR thinking TRULY drives your life. The world we live in is created by the thoughts we think. Are you in the driver's seat or the passenger seat of your destiny? Who is behind **your** steering wheel? The hardest thing for people to learn is that they are the total sum of their thoughts.

Think about it. Your thinking truly drives your life. You should be present with your thoughts. What does *'present with your thoughts'* mean? Living in the present moment, being in touch with your present thoughts, not yesterday's thoughts or tomorrow's thoughts. Eight words that can change your life. *'Your life is what your thoughts make it.'*

You can control what you think. For example, tell yourself that you feel **TERRIFIC**. That you feel **HAPPY**. That you feel **HEALTHY**. Every day, tell yourself you feel **TERRIFIC, HAPPY & HEALTHY**. I know you might not feel like it all the time, but did you know that if you repeat something for 30 days, it becomes a habit. You will start to form a new habit without even realising it.

If someone asks, 'How are you feeling?' Say, **TERRIFIC** even if you don't feel like it, because:

THOUGHTS become **ACTIONS**
ACTIONS form **HABITS**
HABITS then become a part of your **CHARACTER**
this is WHO you Aspire to be!

'We are what we repeatedly do;
Excellence, then, is not an act, but a HABIT.' **Aristotle**

You should see the reaction I get when people ask me 'How are you feeling today?' With *gusto*, I say, **'Terrific, thanks.'**

Be careful of your thoughts,
for your thoughts become your words.

Be careful of your words,
for your words become your actions.

Be careful of your actions,
for your actions become your habits.

Be careful of your habits,
for your habits become your character.

Be careful of your character,
for your character becomes your destiny.

Chinese Proverb

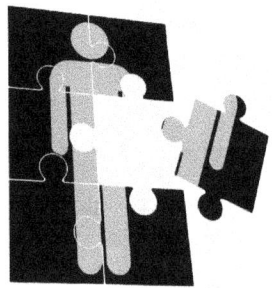

So how about concentrating your thoughts on **THE PRESENT** rather than dwelling on the past and/or thinking about the future? It's okay to plan for the future but we are not there yet. Living for **NOW** will help you have a better future. Every day we are confronted with choices, so I would encourage you to look at the following illustration of flagpoles, standing side by side, as a metaphor for a more focused life.

Forget the Past ⚑ **Focus on the Present** ⚑ The Future, it's a Mystery!

For the beach goers - 'Always swim between the flags.'

Why waste energy on the past and on the future, when instead you could **increase your energy** levels dramatically by simply focusing your thoughts on **THE PRESENT**.

The Past is History
The Future is a Mystery
Today is a gift - that's why they call it 'THE PRESENT'

There is no *time* like THE PRESENT. Keep focused on it and use your energy wisely. We are not on this earth for a long time.

Did you know that the **average** person lives for approximately 29,200 DAYS? (80 years) *Time* is short. Work out how many days you have left – it's easy. The following is based on the average lifespan of 80 years:

80 years of life minus your current age = how many years you have left
For example: 80 – 15 = 65
How many years you have left times days in a year = how many days you have left
For example: 65 x 365 = 23,725

When you look at it from this angle, you really start to appreciate how important it is to make every single day count.

Now you can see how important it is to start living each day with a purpose ensuring that you make the most of each moment. How your life turns out is not based on other people. It is based on how you use your time, knowledge, and skills in any environment, to create the quality of life that you desire and you deserve, *and help others to do the same*.

SO, who decides if you have a GREAT day, every day?
YOU DO! YES, YOU!
It's not anyone else's responsibility.

Did you know that we have at least 80,000 thoughts every day?

Unfortunately, 95% of those thoughts are the same as yesterday. We are always thinking about yesterday or tomorrow, but what about today? <u>What about now?</u> Understand that **your thoughts determine your actions.**

Let me ask you - What kind of thoughts are you thinking? Are your thoughts contaminated or pure? Remember, you control what you think.

Thinking like a winner is the first step to living like a winner. As mentioned, you become what you think about most of the time. You are the architect of your personality and character. So, why not become the person who thinks, *I can achieve?*

People succeed not because they have remarkable characteristics or qualities. They succeed due to their willingness to grow and want more from life. But remember, most successful people start out as quite ordinary, just like you and me. The turning point comes when we begin to believe what we have in ourselves, that spark, that can lead us onward and upward to the accomplishment of anything that we really want in life.

If you think you're beaten, you are.
If you think you dare not, you don't.
If you would like to win, but think you can't.
It's almost a cinch you won't.

Life's battles don't always go
to the stronger or faster man.
But sooner or later the man, who wins,
is the man who thinks *he can!*

'The Man Who Thinks He Can' by Walter D. Wintle

Remember, you have nothing to deal with but your own thoughts.

No matter what problem you may have to face today, there is a solution, because **you have nothing to deal with but your own thoughts.** You have the power to select and control your thoughts. *Thoughts.* Write this word down. Have it on your desk. Hang it in your bedroom. Write it in your diary. It will transform your life. *Thoughts! Thoughts! Thoughts!*

Training your thoughts, it's not easy, but it's worth it. Train yourself to stay focused about your thinking at any given time. You think, and your thoughts become reality, all unknown to yourself. You are weaving the pattern of your own destiny, here and now, by the way in which you allow yourself to think, day by day and all day long. Don't allow your thoughts to wander. If you constantly allow your mind to wander, you might as well give up all hope of shaping your life into what you want it to be. **Your thoughts are your focus.** Do you constantly find yourself thinking about what I need to do next rather than focusing on the present and what you are actually doing? So many of us unconsciously do this that consequently we lose control of our thoughts by letting them runaway.

What about the negative thoughts? Negative thoughts will come to you all day long. The negative things in your mind – the fears, doubts, resentments – are to be starved out of existence by refusing to feed them with your attention. These things do not matter if you don't entertain those thoughts. You have the power to select and control your thoughts. When you catch yourself thinking a negative thought, make the decision to change it into a different and more positive thought.

Negative thinking can have a strong and sometimes devastating impact on all aspects of our lives. Negative thoughts serve no real purpose and it automatically causes negative emotions (emotions reflect our thoughts that are felt in the body). Most negative thoughts flow from two directions. First, they come from dwelling on the past and feeling guilty about something you said or did. Second, they come from dwelling on the future in fear of what may or may not happen for yourself and others. See if you can catch negative thoughts as they arise, before they gain too much momentum.

Become a watcher of your thoughts. To become free of negative thinking, you must learn to become more aware of your thoughts. Pay more attention to what is going on inside your mind. This can be achieved by living in the present moment. Become a curious observer of what goes on in your inner environment. Be in charge of your thoughts. You are the product of all your thoughts and actions.

Start to generate positive thoughts and feelings of self-worth and acceptance in place of old thoughts of inferiority and failure. Keep your thoughts focused in the present instead of living in the past or future. You are the captain of your life. You choose your attitude. You are responsible for your own happiness or unhappiness. You are in the driver's seat of your destiny, not the passenger.

Choose positive thoughts, and eliminate negative ones. Negative excuses will keep you from reaching your potential. Negative thoughts produce negative lives. Positive thoughts produce positive lives. As I said before, it's not easy. You might wish to try this, as it worked for me.

> Place a rubber band around your wrist (either one) and every time you find your mind wandering or thinking negative thoughts, *ping* the rubber band against your wrist. Ouch! Yes, I know, it hurts! However, there is only so much *pinging* one can cope with before you start focusing again.

It's called conscious thinking.

I'm sure you will be able to think of ways to stop this negative chitchat going on within. **Attention is the key to life.** Where your attention is, there is your destiny.

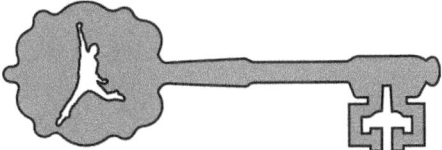

Since we are what we believe, and our lives and circumstances reflect to us what we believe – changing our thinking does change our lives. If you really want to change your world, you need to change your thinking. Choose your thoughts wisely, as there is great power in your thoughts. Your thoughts carry with them chain reactions –like a stone that is thrown into a pond, causing ripple effects.

Your Life Is What Your Thoughts Make It!

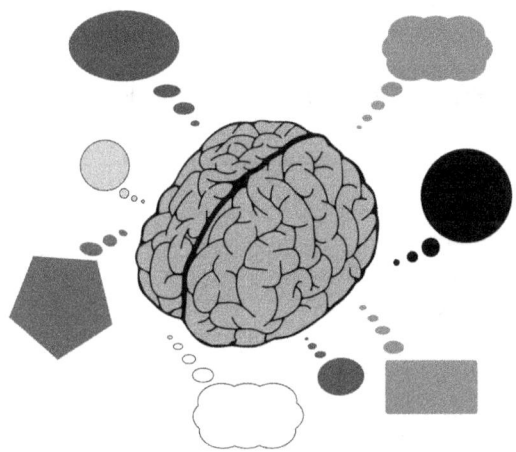

♪**Let's get started by challenging your thoughts. It won't be easy, but ask yourself whether you want to be a prisoner of the past or a pioneer of the future. Remember, you have nothing to deal with, but your own thoughts.**

What are your thoughts? Write them down and get them out of your head.

- Maybe you have some goals you want to achieve.
- What are the special talents or interests you want to pursue? It doesn't matter where your talent lies — whether it's in drama, cooking, music — when you do something that you like doing and have a talent for it, it's exhilarating.
- You may have a gift for being creative, a fast learner or a good leader.

Write your thoughts down. This will enable you to sort through and solve them with focus. To prioritise your thoughts, you should number them and work through them in that order. Also, you may wish to redo and renumber this list on a regular basis by deleting what you have finished and adding more thoughts.

Date	Priority	Positive thoughts +	Negative thoughts -

Dated: __/__/__

**_Training your thoughts...it's not easy,
but it's worth it._**

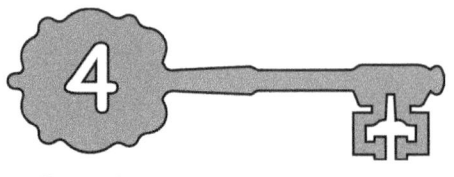

Attitude Is Everything!

'People may hear your words, but they feel your attitude.'
John C. Maxwell

One of the greatest gifts you possess as a human being is **YOUR ATTITUDE**. You own it. You control it. You are responsible for it and you can change it anytime. Your attitude is not dependent on your surroundings and most importantly, not excusable when it is terrible.

Attitude is the way you think. Your attitude is something other people can see. They see it in the way you move, hear it in your voice, and feel it when they are with you. Your attitude expresses itself in everything you do, all the time wherever you are.

Just imagine yourself walking down a dark alley way in New York, alone. You are feeling a little uneasy but it is the only way to reach your destination. Whether you realise it or not, right here, right now, YOU choose your *ATTITUDE*. Let me explain.

(1) **Negative attitude** would be having your back hunched over in fear, looking over your shoulder to see if someone is following you, walking so fast that you nearly trip over! This displays an attitude of negativity.

(2) **Positive attitude** is to stand tall, walk with confidence as if you are in control and know where you are heading (hopefully you do). It's so simple; it's all in our *ATTITUDE*, even the way we walk. Please let this sink in, it's such an important truth.

A negative attitude always invites negative results. A positive attitude always invites positive results.

Attitude makes a difference every hour, every day in everything you do for your entire life. What **YOU** get out of each thing you do will equal the attitude you have when you do it. Anything that **YOU** do with a negative attitude will work against you. Anything that **YOU** do with a positive attitude will work for you.

If you have a positive attitude, you are looking for ways to solve problems and you are letting go of things over which you have *no* control. You can develop a positive attitude by emphasising the good, by being tough minded and by refusing defeat.

Your attitude dictates your performance in life. Champions work at doing things most people are not willing to do. It's your attitude that usually determines how well you handle any circumstance. Right thinking is vital to successful living — *as you think, so you are*.

What kind of attitude do you have?

Attitude is a mental outlook, a frame of mind. It's how we think. Attitude is the reflection of the person inside. It is what goes on inside of us – thoughts and feelings – about ourselves, others and life in general. Attitude is a choice – the most important one you will ever make. It affects everything you do in life. Attitude is far more important than intelligence, education, special talent, or luck.

Your daily conversations mirror your attitude. If you continuously say and think positive things, you are reinforcing your positive self-esteem and self-image. Also, repeated negative statements defeat your efforts. Having a positive attitude, a positive outlook, and a positive approach to life can make such a difference to your day.

A person with a poor attitude becomes a magnet for unpleasant experiences. When those experiences come – as they will, because of this attitude – they tend to reinforce their poor attitude, thereby bringing more problems, and so on. This person becomes an example of self-generating, doom-fulfilling prophecy. And it's all a matter – believe it or not – of attitude. We get what we expect.

Destructive emotions, such as anger, hatred, and jealousy don't only hurt others; they hurt you to a greater degree. They can make your life miserable. They can make you sick. Forgive everyone who has ever hurt you – really forgive them – and then forgive yourself. That's all past. Stewing over it, can only make you sick. Get rid of it and rise above that sort of thing. You are better than that, but for many people this is their **biggest** challenge in life.

For example, take the lesson of the 'Two Wolves' (Anger)
(Author Unknown)

An Indian grandfather once offered advice to his grandson. The boy had come to the old man after being betrayed by a friend. They sat around a fire under the open starry sky. *'Let me tell you a story.'* The old man began, *'I too, at times, have felt a great hate for those that have taken so much, with no sorrow for what they have done.'*

The grandfather looked at his grandson and said. *'But hate wears you down and does not hurt your enemy. It is like taking poison and wishing your enemy would die. I have struggled with these feelings many times.'* He continued, *'It is as if there are two wolves inside me.'*

'One is good and does no harm.' The grandfather continues. *'He lives in harmony with everything around him, and does not take offence when no offence was intended. He will only fight when it is right to do so, and in the right way.'*

'But the other wolf, ah! He is full of anger.' The grandfather said with intensity. *'The littlest thing will set him into a fit of temper. He fights everyone, all the time, for no reason. He cannot think because his anger and hate are so great. It is helpless anger, for his anger will change nothing.'*

'Sometimes, it is hard to live with these two wolves inside me, for both of them try to dominate my spirit.' The grandfather finished. The boy looked intently into his grandfather's eyes and asked. *'Which one wins, Grandfather?'*

The grandfather smiled and quietly said, *'The one I feed.'*

This is such a powerful story: so simple and yet so true. I think each one of us has these two wolves running around inside us. The angry wolf or the good wolf is fed daily by the choices we make with our thoughts. What you think about and dwell upon will appear in your life and influence your behaviour. We have a choice. If we feed the good wolf, it will show up in our character, habits and behaviour positively. If we feed the angry wolf, our whole world will turn negative. Like poison, this will slowly eat away at our soul.

The crucial question is, "Which wolf are you feeding today?"

The Good Wolf   The Angry Wolf

How does one develop a good attitude? The same way one develops any other ability: through practice! I have a saying displayed in many places around my home and I would like to share it with you. You will find one like it at the back of this book. Please feel free to make copies and share as you like. ***'Your future will be bright, if your attitude is right.'*** Why not take a screenshot on your phone? Or maybe stick it on the bathroom mirror, so you'll see it first thing every morning. Place it wherever you spend a great deal of your time.

Most people never think about their attitudes at all. For most of them, it's a matter of beginning each day in neutral. Their attitudes are neither good nor bad. In this way, they are allowing the environment to determine their attitude and mood for them, rather than making their own conscious choice.

As soon as a person begins to change their attitude, and their thinking, their surroundings will also change. It works like this:

Great attitude = Great results
Good attitude = Good results
Fair or average attitude = Fair or average results
Poor attitude = Poor results

We have the ability to shape our own lives.

Over the years, I have found myself using two words that have worked for me: grateful and enthusiasm. I am grateful for the opportunity to live on this beautiful and astounding planet Earth, and each morning I wake up with enthusiasm to what the day will bring. I know the world will give back to me what I put out, in the way of attitude, so it's up to me. I'm responsible as are you.

Whoever coined the cliché 'Life's too short' certainly knew what they were talking about. It really is too short – much too short – to spend any of our valuable time mimicking the attitudes of others, especially if they are negative. A great attitude does much more than brighten our world; it seems to magically connect us to all sorts of opportunities, and maybe that's what people mean when they say we are lucky.

Suddenly, we do find ourselves getting the so-called 'breaks.' But it's really nothing more than this new connection to the world that comes with a great attitude. We find ourselves doing more in what seems to be less time, because of our attitude. We put ourselves directly in the path of all kinds of wonderful happenings.

You can do yourself a great kindness simply by keeping promises to yourself, by keeping up with your grades or looking for a part-time job. This positive attitude will help with your self-confidence. As you develop a great attitude, you'll probably realise that you've already placed yourself on the road to the incredible awesome you. You are well on your way.

A	**Always make today your best day**
T	**Take pride in a job well done**
T	**Treat others with respect**
I	**Isolate your negative thoughts**
T	**Treat tasks as opportunities**
U	**Utilise your talents everyday**
D	**Do the job right the first time**
E	**Expect positive outcomes daily**

🔖 Let's get started by answering the following questions.
Please answer them honestly.

What does it take to have a positive attitude?

_____
_____
_____
_____
_____
_____
_____
_____
_____
_____
_____
_____

How would I describe my attitude?

_____
_____
_____
_____
_____
_____
_____
_____
_____
_____
_____
_____

What can I do to improve my attitude?

_____
_____
_____
_____
_____
_____
_____
_____
_____
_____
_____
_____

Mornings are extremely important. It is the groundwork from which the day is built. How you choose to spend your morning can easily show what kind of day you are going to have. Keep in mind, it's not what happens to you, it is what you do about it. A positive attitude can make all the difference. Think about the following questions.

1. **What is the most important thing I can do today for my own well-being?**

   Every day is another chance to change your life. If you need to work on your attitude, work on it. Figure out how you can improve yourself today.

   Perhaps start with a positive statement, repeat it often. For example, 'Every day in every way, I'm getting better, better and better.' Walk tall – be proud and confident. Smile – a smile can make someone's day. Acknowledge others and take the time to listen to them. Make every day count.

2. **What can I do to make a positive difference in the lives around me?**

   Evaluate your attitude towards the people around you. Learn what matters most to others and practice it. There are many small, simple actions you can do to impact the people around you, your community and the world. So, do your best to leave everything you touch today, a little better than you found it.

3. **What would I like to remember at the end of each day? Write it down. Do you have a journal? If not, it's a great time to get one.**

What did I do today that is worth remembering?

_____

_____

Did I try something new? If so, what?

_____

_____

Who did I share my new found positive attitude with?

_____

_____

Did I walk my talk? If so, how?

_____

_____

I want to share a story with you, as this story has had a major impact on my life, and I share it with the hope that you will take something away from it. **This is attitude at its greatest!**

Jerry is the manager of a restaurant. He is always in a good mood.
When someone would ask him how he was doing, he would always reply, '*If I were any better, I would be twins!*'
Many of the waiters at his restaurant quit their jobs when he changed jobs, so they could follow him around from restaurant to restaurant.
Why?
Because, Jerry was a natural motivator.
If an employee was having a bad day, Jerry was always there, telling the employee how to look on the positive side of the situation.

Seeing this style really made me curious, so one day I went up to Jerry and asked him, 'I don't get it'!
Jerry replied, '*Each morning, I wake up and say to myself, 'I have two choices today. I can choose to be in a good mood or I can choose to be in a bad mood. I always choose to be in a good mood*'.
Each time something bad happens, I can choose to be a victim, or I can choose to learn from it. Every time someone comes to me complaining, I can choose to accept their complaining, or I can point out the positive side of life. I always choose the positive side of life.'

'But it's not always that easy', I protested.
'*Yes, it is*', Jerry said.
'*Life is all about choices. When you cut away all the junk, every situation is a choice. You choose how you react to situations. You choose how people will affect your mood. You choose to be in a good mood or bad mood.*
It's your choice how you live your life.'

Several years later, I heard that Jerry accidentally did something you are never supposed to do in the restaurant business.
He left the back door of his restaurant open.
And then...

In the morning, he was robbed by three armed men.

While Jerry was trying to open the safe box, his hand, shaking from nervousness, slipped off the combination.

The robbers panicked and shot him.

Luckily, Jerry was found quickly and rushed to the hospital.

After 18 hours of surgery and weeks of intensive care,

Jerry was released from the hospital with fragments of the bullets still in his body.

I saw Jerry about six months after the accident.

When I asked him how he was, he replied,

'If I were any better, I'd be twins. Want to see my scars?'

I declined to see his wounds, but did ask him what had gone through his mind as the robbery took place.

'The first thing that went through my mind was that I should have locked the back door,' Jerry replied.

'Then, after they shot me, as I lay on the floor, I remembered that I had **two choices:**

I could choose to live, or I could choose to die. I chose to live.'

'Weren't you scared', I asked?

Jerry continued, 'The paramedics were great. They kept telling me I was going to be fine. But when they wheeled me into the emergency room and I saw the expression on the faces of the doctors and nurses, I got really scared. In their eyes, I read 'He's a dead man.'

I knew I needed to take action.'

'What did you do?' I asked.

'Well, there was a big nurse shouting questions at me,' said Jerry.

'She asked if I was allergic to anything. 'Yes,' I replied.

The doctors and nurses stopped working as they waited for my reply.

I took a deep breath and yelled, *'Bullets!'*

Over their laugher, I told them, *'I am choosing to live.*

Please operate on me as is I am alive, not dead.'

Jerry lived, thanks to the skill of his doctors, but also because of his **AMAZING ATTITUDE.**

I learned from him that every day you have the choice to either enjoy life or to hate it. The only thing that is truly yours – that no one can control or take from you – is your **ATTITUDE**.

So, if you can take care of that, everything else in life becomes much easier.

Now you have two choices to make.

You always have two choices.

Attitude is a choice!

Enough for today.
Tomorrow's going to be even better!

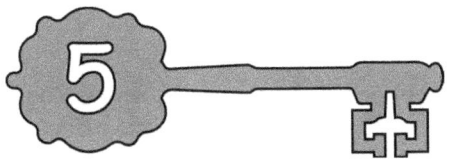

Daily Mental Vitamins!

'The secret to change is to focus all of your energy, not fighting the old, but on building the new.'
Socrates

Remember the last key, when I mentioned that mornings are extremely important as it is the groundwork from which the day is built? Let's hone into that now. How you choose to spend your mornings can be used to predict what kind of day you are going to have. Realise, that the one thing you have absolute control over, is your attitude. Again, a positive attitude can make all the difference.

Do you take vitamins? If so, how much are you paying for them? I'll let you in on a little secret. The daily vitamins I take are FREE. Yes, FREE! There are many vitamins but only seven vitamins are important to me. Before I put my feet on the ground each morning, I do a mental vitamin check starting with

A CHECK-UP FROM THE NECK UP!

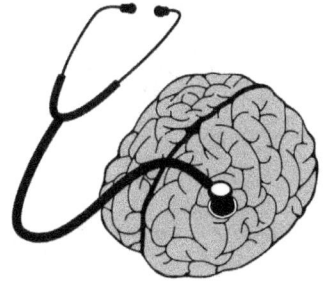

Vitamin 'A' ATTITUDE

So, I ask myself: what is my attitude going to be today? I have a **choice,** either negative or positive. Of course, I would choose positive, who wouldn't?

So, I start my day with a positive **ATTITUDE** and the day seems to be a great one. I notice that people around me seem happier and their energy levels are so motivating. So, live each day to the fullest. It's the best time to be alive!

If on the other hand, I just jump out of bed without checking my attitude, I can assure you nine times out of ten, my day is nowhere near as positive. Why? It's so easy to go with the flow, and that is what happens. I just let whatever comes along during the day affect my attitude whether negative or positive, as I did not take the time to inject myself with my daily mental vitamins.

Remember, there is little difference in people, but the little difference makes a big difference. The little difference is **ATTITUDE!** The big difference is whether it is negative or positive.

Vitamin A Example: Somehow you forget to bring your pencil case to School/TAFE/College/University. You have a choice. You can choose to be in a bad mood all day, putting yourself down for being forgetful and careless. Or you can choose to laugh about it, instead being excited at the chance to meet new people, as you ask them to borrow a pencil in each class. See the effect that it has on those around you. Appreciate every moment and take from it everything that you possibly can, for you may never be able to experience it again.

Vitamin 'B' BELIEF

What do you believe in for the day ahead? It's about making conscious choices about who you are. To believe in yourself, and know that you can achieve whatever you desire, without the need for proof or evidence.

So, I start my day with a positive **BELIEF**, which could be working towards an idea, an understanding of myself and others, or simply having certainty in myself. When I say, 'certainty in myself,' it's because I know how powerful our thoughts are; our life is the expression of our thinking. It can be a blessing, or a curse, it's entirely up to you.

Remember, your **BELIEF**/focus determines your reality. You get exactly what you BELIEVE/focus on – nothing more, nothing less. Tell yourself you are a great individual and believe in yourself, for if you don't believe in yourself, no one else will believe in you. People will always take you at your own valuation which simply means, the value that you really put on yourself. It's important, really important, to believe in yourself as you are the creator of your own world. **Have faith in yourself.**

Vitamin B Example: You hear a rumour going around about yourself. Someone has started telling other people that you're not a nice person. If you have belief and confidence in yourself, you will know that this is **not** true, and you will be able to ignore the untrue things that other people are saying about you. Believe and trust in yourself, and not in the words of others. Hold your head up high because you have every right to.

Vitamin 'C' COURAGE

The root of the word courage is *cor*—the Latin word for heart. 'To speak one's mind, by telling all one's heart.' *(Brene Brown)*. Are **you** courageous?

Ordinary courage is about putting our weaknesses on the line. In today's world, that's extra-ordinary. Courage is not something we have or don't have, it's something we practice.

So, I start my day with **COURAGE** by working on having confidence in myself. Having confidence grows slowly from the inside out. I know it takes practice to be confident in who you are, what you have achieved and the direction you are going in. But it's worth it.

Courage is huge in my life. I'm praying for some, feeling grateful for having found a little bit, appreciating it in other people, or studying it. I don't think that makes me exceptional. Everyone wants to be brave. **Don't you?**

Remember, nothing will change if you don't. Dare to be different. Have courage. **COURAGE** is being ***BRAVE*** without being overcome by ***FEAR.***

Vitamin C Example: Since courage is something that needs to be practiced, start with something small. Put your hand up and answer any questions that you think you know the answer to. Even if you get it wrong, at least you tried. Try and do something that you've always wanted to do, but have held yourself back. Maybe you were worried about failing or making a mistake. We learn from our mistakes. But have courage and just try. You will often surprise yourself with the results. And even if you don't quite get there, you still tried and learnt something new, and can be comfortable knowing that you have done your best. *'Shoot for the moon. Even if you miss, you'll land amongst the stars.'*

Vitamin 'D' DETERMINATION

Have you decided on what you want to achieve today or are you just going along aimlessly? Choose a destination with purpose. You were born for a purpose and your greatest challenge is to discover it and immerse yourself in it. Determination equals strength of mind, character and willpower.

So, I start my day with **DETERMINATION**, focusing on my purpose of making a difference to whomever I meet. Whether it is with words of encouragement, a hug or just a warm friendly smile. A smile is a curved line that sets things straight.

A sincere smile makes others feel good. The power of a sincere smile is incredible. Did you know that a smile stimulates the thymus gland which is located below your throat, which then produces endorphins (happy feelings)? So, when you smile, you will start to feel happier inside. Give it a go.

My purpose is to help make everyone's day a happier one, just with a simple smile. When I'm out and about I notice that many people don't seem to smile, that is why **I AM DETERMINED** to put a smile on everyone's dial because I understand how important a smile can be. It affects your whole body (as mentioned above) from the skin right into the skeleton, including all blood vessels, nerves, and muscles.

A fantastic grin can lift almost anyone's spirit, and single-handedly change the mood of a room. I think smiles are like boomerangs, if you throw one, it should come back. To me, a smile says:

> I like you.
> You make me happy.
> I'm so glad to see you.
> It says that you are in control.
> It says that you're confident.

A smile is an investment. Last year's smiles are paying you dividends today.

Remember, be determined to make a difference by focusing on your purpose. This simple act can change your day.

Vitamin D Example: What is your aim for today? What is it that you are determined to achieve? Do you want to show courage and introduce yourself to a potential new friend? Do you want to push yourself to try a little bit harder in life, with anything you are struggling with? Do you want to have a good attitude, choosing to focus on the good that surrounds you, rather than the bad? So many things to think about! Right?

Soon, you will start to realise that if you hadn't pushed yourself by overcoming those struggles, you would have never realised your potential, strength and willpower. Without these small challenges, life would be like a smooth, paved, straight, flat road to **NOWHERE**. Safe and comfortable, but dull and totally pointless.

Vitamin 'E' ENTHUSIASM

It's my favourite vitamin! The word 'enthusiasm' has its root in the Greek language; literally it means 'the God (entheo) inside (iasm)'. It is the 'Life Energy' that flows freely through you, if you dare to be yourself. It is the trembling you feel when you take the risk of being yourself.

So, I start my day with **ENTHUSIASM by acting enthusiastically and then I become enthusiastic**. Over the years so many people have asked me 'What are you on? Can I have some too?' Yes, you sure can! It's my daily mental vitamins with a double dose of enthusiasm. Watch out – it's contagious! The world evolves thanks to the drive of strongly motivated and enthusiastic people.

So, what is enthusiasm?

Enthusiasm is like a fire, burning everything in its path and igniting the fuse of achievement. Enthusiasm is what drives us to create and to accomplish things.

Enthusiasm can be seen in the twinkling of your eyes, the determination in your step, the power in your hands, the irresistible energy that pulls you to what you have decided to create. It's the amazing engine of life.

Ralph Waldo Emerson wrote: *'Nothing great was ever achieved without enthusiasm.'* I SAY YES TO THAT! With it, anything can be achieved. Enthusiasm can change the world. Enthusiasm is a wave coming from the heart that lifts you up and takes you along.

Remember, bring enthusiasm to everything you do. Enthusiasm is to your life what electricity is to a light bulb. Nothing happens until you flip the switch. With this newfound enthusiasm for life, you can influence the people around you as there will always be an opportunity to turn on a small light in a dark room, thus changing peoples' lives.

Vitamin E Example: Have you ever noticed that during Christmas and the New Year, we seem to have this overwhelming enthusiasm and excitement for life? Do you agree? Why don't we try and have this enthusiasm and excitement for life, every day of the year?

Get started on the road to enthusiasm by taking a moment to stop and think about how far you have already come on this journey to change. You are making a difference to yourself and soon the people around you will certainly feel your energy. How exciting is that? You are already making a difference in the world.

Make the choice to be enthusiastic about your day, every day. Get enthusiastic about the changes you are now creating, towards becoming the incredible awesome you.

**Enthusiasm is to your life
what electricity is to a light bulb.**

Nothing happens until you flip the switch!

Vitamin 'F' FORGIVENESS - understanding, compassion, and tolerance are some synonyms.

Forgiveness is a choice and has nothing whatsoever to do with the other person. Forgiveness has everything to do with the person forgiving. It's a decision we make for ourselves. We tend to think of forgiveness as an act of kindness that we choose to give to someone. In reality, we are actually giving that gift to ourselves. It is an act of kindness for our own well-being. We must learn to forgive so we can feel better and move on. We receive the reward of our forgiveness of others with FREEDOM!

So, how do I start my day with **FORGIVENESS?** Simply by forgiving myself for whatever I did yesterday. I'm quite serious about this. We usually wake up with thoughts about ourselves and what we did yesterday, especially the senseless thoughts of 'Why did I do that? Gosh, why did I say that? I feel so guilty!' Then you start to feel negative about yourself and this can be the start of another miserable day. STOP! Don't be a victim, free yourself. A free person must act freely, openly and lovingly. A victim claims the right to be angry.

I wasted so many mornings, days, weeks and even years playing the victim. Why? I didn't know any better until I gained a true understanding of forgiveness. I finally realised that I had to learn to forgive myself in order to forgive others.

Nearly all of us have been hurt by the actions or words of others. Maybe your parents or friends criticised you for something and you are still carrying these wounds which leave you with feelings of anger or even bitterness. If you don't practice forgiveness, you can be the one who pays most deeply. But by embracing forgiveness, you can also embrace peace, hope, gratitude and joy. Letting go of grudges and bitterness can make way for happier relationships, less anxiety, stress and resentment.

Remember, when you truly forgive you remember nothing about what has been wrongly done to you. You forgive and move on, you remember no more. Easier said than done, I know. Living life without forgiveness is like drinking poison and waiting for the other person to die. Being able to forgive means you are also able to move forward.

Vitamin F Example: Learn to let go. A great way to do this is to learn a form of meditation. A simple way to mediate is to sit quietly, upright in a chair and focus on your breathing. Simply follow the rise and fall of your chest. Close your eyes and become aware of your body. Notice the thoughts that come and go.

This is a great way to stop your mind from working overtime and constantly dwelling on the hurt and the anger. Sign up for a yoga class and see if it resonates with you. Spend time alone, give yourself permission to do nothing occasionally. We all need our own space.

Be patient and kind with yourself as it will take time to commence healing. Forgiveness can be a slow process. You will know when forgiveness is complete; when you experience the freedom that comes after the moment you take a deep breath and relax. Your mind is clear. Frequently take deep breaths and discover the benefits of breathing fully.

Vitamin 'G' GRATITUDE – Gratitude simply means being aware of and thankful for the good things that happen; taking time to express thanks.

Sometimes in life, it's easy to focus on all of the negative things happening around us. It's so easy to see what we don't have and what is going wrong. But if we take a moment to stop and clearly look at our surroundings, we might notice that it really isn't that bad. Do you have a home to live in? A warm and comfortable bed to sleep in at night? Family and friends who support you and love you? Are you able to spend time doing things that you enjoy? While your life may not be perfect and may not be exactly how you would like it to be, there is so much around you to be grateful for. Recognising and focusing on what you do have, rather than what you don't have, is one of the easiest ways to find happiness. Taking a moment each day to reflect on what you are grateful for can help put things into perspective and lift your mood.

So, I start my day by simply saying 'thank you'. It's the first thing I do even before I get out of bed. As I begin to wake up I'm being grateful for another day. I hear the birds sing and feel like I am waking up listening to an orchestra, it's amazing. I feel like I am being entertained by Mother Nature. So, it puts a smile on my dial. I feel lucky that I am aware of the sounds around me.

Remember, to be aware of and thankful for the good things that happen; never take them for granted. Maybe you could try to express your gratitude by saying thank you to those around you. Sharing gratitude is a sure-fire way of not only improving your mood but the mood of others around you.

Vitamin G Example: Regardless of your external situation, even if very unfortunate, you can always find something to be grateful for. Why is this true? Because there is always a worse scenario than the one you are in.

Gratitude for what you have, or how lucky you are, is an instant cure for a bad mood. As soon as you realise you can be grateful, your spirit lifts and you begin to see life differently.

Does it mean you are just an unrealistic fool if you are continually grateful?

Some people worry that too much gratitude will blind them to reality. On the contrary, gratitude helps you face reality with a more open mind. You can look at the worst situation, find something to be grateful for, and then proceed to solve the problems in front of you from a more balanced point of view.

Take a dose of gratitude with the knowledge it is the energy behind your words of appreciation which will transform your inner world. A habit of happiness. It's a quick fix to annoying thoughts. It's the antidote for anxiety. It suffocates fear.

Gratitude is contagious, transformative and exponential. Ask yourself the question: 'What am I grateful for, right now?'

GRATITUDE
IS THE BEST ATTITUDE!

In summary, **Daily Mental Vitamins** are one of the keys to change. Nothing will change if YOU don't make a commitment to yourself, by going the extra mile each morning, injecting yourself with daily doses of:

ATTITUDE, BELIEF, COURAGE, DETERMINATION, ENTHUSIASM, FORGIVENESS AND GRATITUDE.

You will be energised with a purpose for the day setting yourself up for great successes. The successes and downfalls (yes downfalls too) that you experience will create who you are, and from these experiences you can learn, helping you grow in wisdom. Easier said than done – I know.

When something goes wrong, turn it into an opportunity to learn something you didn't know, especially about yourself. When something goes wrong for someone else, turn it into an opportunity to be kind and supportive.

You will be so surprised how a small commitment of injecting yourself with daily doses of mental vitamins, can change your life! So, change it, create it, own it and love it!

🎧 Before we move forward, take some time to write down your daily intake of Vitamins - **A**ttitude, **B**elief, **C**ourage, **D**etermination, **E**nthusiasm, **F**orgiveness and **G**ratitude.

What did you do about your Vitamin Attitude today?

_____
_____
_____
_____
_____
_____
_____

How did that make you feel?

_____
_____
_____
_____
_____
_____
_____

What did you do about your Vitamin Belief today?

_____
_____
_____
_____
_____
_____
_____

How did that make you feel?

_____
_____
_____
_____
_____
_____
_____

What did you do about your Vitamin Courage today?

_____
_____
_____
_____

How did that make you feel?

_____
_____
_____
_____

What did you do about your Vitamin Determination today?

_____
_____
_____
_____

How did that make you feel?

_____
_____
_____
_____

What did you do about your Vitamin Enthusiasm today?

_____
_____
_____
_____

How did that make you feel?

_____
_____
_____
_____
_____

What did you do about your Vitamin Forgiveness today?

_____
_____
_____
_____
_____

How did that make you feel?

_____
_____
_____
_____
_____

What did you do about your Vitamin Gratitude today?

_____
_____
_____
_____
_____

How did that make you feel?

_____
_____
_____
_____
_____
_____ Dated: __/__/___

'The food you feed your mind determines the future of your life.'

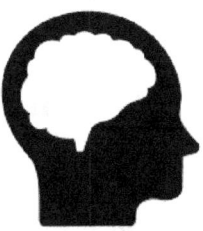

Rest up. Take it all in.

Make those vitamins work for you and start to see the change in the world around you.

Words for Growth!

'Be impeccable with your word.'
Don Miguel Ruiz

Gosh I love words! I have such an appreciation for the English language, which I believe comes from my diverse background. Growing up, my parents taught me to speak in their native languages of German and Serbian. English was originally a foreign language for me, and was a barrier when trying to fit into school and the local community. By the time I started school, I was behind everyone else and learning was a struggle. But throughout my life I have always done my best to convert this struggle into a passion. I now love the English language and relish the opportunity to help students expand their vocabulary and express themselves with newfound passion.

When I went to TAFE to study Shorthand/Typing, my teacher asked if I had difficulty understanding English. For example, one day he checked my shorthand outline – the word in question was 'specific' and my shorthand was 'Pacific', as in the ocean. I had never heard of, or understood the word 'specific' until that very day. **Thus, the dictionary became my best friend.**

I've learnt that **the right words** can take you by the hand and lead you to a more fulfilling life. It's about putting your energies into the right beliefs – **the right words**. We are all brought up with different backgrounds, so we need to be aware of others beliefs when communicating. What might not seem hurtful to us, maybe very hurtful to others.

I've also learnt that the ***wrong words can lead you down the path to average***. The wrong words lead to wrong choices, and wrong results.

In your life simple words are reflected in your beliefs. From there they shape your days, months and years. Words have a surprisingly profound effect on just how you lead your life. Does it really work? Almost without fail. And your life is proof that it works. Here's just one simple example.

What day of the week are you happiest and most energetic? Which day brings you the most success and rewards? Most people answer Fridays. Why? Friday is the entrance to the weekend. Mention the word Monday and it brings out negative emotions, whereas people tend to reveal their happiness when the word Friday is mentioned. Words can be powerful. Just how powerful are your words?

A great example is when Martin Luther King Jr. brought an entire nation together as he began his historic speech with, **'I have a dream.'** Words are a force and it gave him the power to express and communicate; and thereby created an historical event.

Words are **so** powerful that one word can transform or destroy a life.

Unfortunately, we aren't fully aware that the words we speak become the house we live in. Through our words, we create our own life, whether negative or positive. Always remember, words are so powerful and have a force, for either good or bad. *It's worth repeating; words are so powerful and have a force, for either good or bad.*

The human mind can be likened to a fertile ground where seeds are continually being planted. The word is like a seed. You plant a seed, a thought, and it grows. Seeds are ideas, beliefs and attitudes. I remember when I was growing up and someone called me 'stupid' and I started to believe it. It took many years to turn that thought around, because I didn't have anyone to tell me otherwise. That is the power of the word. Please think about the seeds/words you are planting every day and the impact it can have on yourself and others.

My advice, guard your tongue, as you cannot unsay a cruel word. Beware of gossip – letting the cat out of the bag is a whole lot easier than putting it back in again!

Not only do others hurt us with their words, did you know that we also use words against ourselves? Most of the time we say negative things like, 'Oh I'm getting old. I'm stupid, I never understand anything. I'm not good enough and I'm never going to be perfect.' And so on. Can you see that?

Seriously, we must start to understand what the word *is* and what the word *does*. When you begin to understand the importance of your words, you will begin to see changes happening in your life. Awesome changes begin to take place. Firstly, in the way you speak with yourself, and later in the way you communicate with other people, especially those you love the most.

Be mindful of your words. Speak with integrity, say only what you mean. Use your words wisely by starting with yourself. Yes, it will take practice, but it's worth it. Remember, the right words can take you by the hand and lead you to a more fulfilling and rewarding life.

The following are a few words you should either get rid of or add to the vocabulary of your daily communications.

Words to Forget	Words to Remember
I can't	I can
I'll try	I will
I have to	I want to
Problem	Opportunity
Difficult	Challenging
Stressed	Motivated
Someday	Today
It's impossible	It's possible
It can't be done	Yes, it can
What if it doesn't work	Try again

Remember things do not change; we change.

As mentioned, choose your words wisely, as **there is great power in your words.**

WORDS HAVE POWER

Have you heard of Kirk Douglas, a famous actor? (He's the father of Michael Douglas).

He was born in 1916 and still alive today (2019).

He once told a story about when he was young and trying to break into acting. He was working as a waiter at the time. After work, he would meet with his friends who were also trying to get into the entertainment business. They met near a couple of benches in Central Park, New York where they would discuss their day and their activities in regards to getting their foot in the door in the entertainment business.

Kirk said that most of the time they were very positive and optimistic, but on one occasion, when he arrived late one night, he found that just about everyone in the group was very negative and depressed. They were talking about quitting. Giving up the idea of making it as an entertainer, and just settling for any job.

Kirk said *'You guys do what you want but I'm not quitting – I'll never stop trying until I make it. I don't care how long it will take. You see that penthouse all lit up, up there? (Pointing to a penthouse in a skyscraper, they all looked up). Someday I'm going to be up there rich and famous and I'm going to look down at this park bench and remember this night.'*

Years later, he was at a party in that penthouse, and he did look down at the park and remembered what he had said one night. He wasn't talking to them at the time – he was talking to himself, making a promise to himself.

The Science of the Spoken Word is – what you say, is what you are eventually going to manifest.

THERE IS GREAT POWER IN YOUR WORDS

🔑 An activity you will find fun and valuable.

Why not think of your mind as a bank account? Every day, make healthy 'deposits' into your account. Here are some suggestions to start filling your account with healthier words:

confident, courageous, forgiving, passionate, optimistic, grateful and whatever other words you believe should go into the box.

Here's an idea on how to make words work for you! Choose a word each day, write it on a piece of paper, and **live** that word for the day. Display the word wherever you need to, to encourage yourself. **Live each of your words**, and step into your awesomeness.

At the end of the day, give thought to how you used that word and happily deposit it into your bank account.

How did that make you feel **?**

_____
_____
_____
_____
_____
_____
_____
_____
_____
_____
_____
_____
_____
_____
_____
_____
_____
_____
_____
_____ Dated: ___/___/___

Stop doubting yourself for everything you're not, and start giving yourself credit for everything you ARE. We must learn to be our own best friend, because sometimes we fall too easily into the trap of being our own worst enemy.

What do you need to stop thinking about and saying to yourself? What are you holding on to that you need to let go of?

I need to:

_____

Dated: __/__/__

BRING LIFE TO YOUR WORDS

Remember when I said, **'the dictionary became my best friend?'** Why not go the extra mile and aim to learn a word a week? Spend time building a powerful vocabulary and amaze your friends with your unusual words. Before you know it, your vocabulary will be powerful and diverse.

Words **O**f **W**isdom!

Here are some very interesting words...

The most *selfish* one-letter word **I**	Avoid it
The most *satisfying* two-letter word **WE**	Use it
The most *poisonous* three-letter word **EGO**	Kill it
The most *used* four-letter word **LOVE**	Value it
The most *pleasing* five-letter word **SMILE**	Keep it
The fastest *spreading* six-letter word **RUMOUR**	Ignore it
The hardest *working* seven-letter word **SUCCESS**	Achieve it
The most *enviable* eight-letter word **JEALOUSY**	Distance it
The most *powerful* nine-letter word **KNOWLEDGE**	Acquire it
The most *essential* ten-letter word **CONFIDENCE**	Trust it

(*Notes I took at a conference, Author Unknown*)

Just how powerful can words be?
Words have a profound effect on how we lead our lives.
The right words lead us to a more fulfilling life.

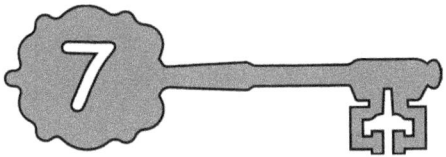

Goals Are Dreams!

'Your goal is to find out who you are.'
A Course In Miracles

Goals are about establishing your dreams. It is **DESIRE**, not ability that determines your success. People with goals succeed because they know where they are going. Living without goals is like going on a trip without a destination. If you don't know where you are going, then you can take any road as it doesn't matter. Any road will get you there.

Successful people have something in common, and that is, they have written goals. Success is not luck. The **key factor** being the overwhelming influence of a written plan. Successful people have an **intense DESIRE** to succeed (just as you have by reading this book) but nothing happens long term without a plan. Don't bank on luck.

If writing **GOALS** is so powerful, why don't more people write them down? The main reasons being:

- People don't know what to do.
- There is a fear of failure.
- There is also fear of success. Questions like: What if I succeed? Will it turn my life around? Will I be out of my comfort zone?
- **PROCRASTINATION** - (the thief of time). It's a silent killer – it grows on you, creeps into your life. The reason we procrastinate, is we believe that taking action would be more painful than doing nothing.

We all start the same way. We get excited about something, a precious dream, we share it with people, but unless we have a plan of action, nothing happens. Nothing happens long term without a plan. So, I encourage you to start crystallising your thinking by using the S.M.A.R.T. acronym, which is a good way to remember the important components of an effective and clear goal.

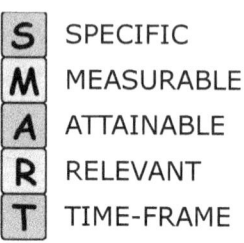

- **Specific:** Be clear on what you want. 'I want better grades' isn't enough. What grade do you want to achieve? The very act of thinking as you write will create a permanent impression in your memory.
- **Measurable:** How will you know when you have achieved your goal? Do you have to wait until the end of semester to receive your exam results? Or can you measure your progress during the term with practice tests?
- **Attainable:** You need to believe that you can reach your goal with real and consistent effort. Keep motivated, move forward step by step until you get there.
- **Relevant:** Your goals should be relevant to your overall purpose, mission and values.
- **Timeframe:** When will you accomplish each of your goals? Specify a time for achieving your objective. This is important in motivating you in the direction of your goal and will keep you moving towards it.

When you set a challenging goal, you'll be further ahead tomorrow than you are today. Even a little can turn out to be a lot! You'll be a happier person.

Stay positive and stay focused. No one can stop you from reaching your **GOALS!**

READY, SET, GOALS!

DREAM BIG

SET GOALS

Have you noticed how negative thinkers avoid setting goals?

- *Goals - who needs them? I'll just wing it, thank you. I prefer to roll with the punches.*
- *I don't want to get trapped by a commitment. Isn't that what happens when you set a goal? I've had enough disappointments.*
- *I don't want to be set up only to be let down. Goals? No more failures, thank you.*

Failure is not a matter of failing to meet your goal. Failure is a matter of not starting towards your goals, and therefore not making the most of the opportunities around you.

***"Shoot for the moon.
Even if you miss, you'll land amongst the stars."***

✒ So, get ready to set goals, and move upwards! ⇗ ⇗ ⇧

We need goals, not for what they get for us, but for what they do for us. Goals are like magnets. They pull us toward them. They are a commitment to do. So, commit to a list. It gives you a method and a structure in achieving what you want out of life.

Goals are important to your future. Pilots need to have a flight plan before lifting off and travelling towards a destination. They must know where they are going, and they need instruments to help guide them to that ultimate destination. Winging it won't work.

Your life is somewhat similar. If you're not going to set goals for yourself, I can assure you that you probably won't make much progress towards the life you really want. So once again, I encourage you to start crystallising your thinking by using the S.M.A.R.T. acronym towards setting effective and clear goals.

Crystallising your goals. All you must do is ask yourself, 'What do I really want?' Say it ALOUD. Then suddenly you will hear yourself say, 'I want this.' Guess what? You will have started the ball rolling on your way to setting a goal. Decide what you want, step forward every day and you will achieve whatever you put your mind to. **Your future is in your hands!**

Limitations - don't compromise when you write your goals. The higher you set your goals, the more concentrated will be your effort to achieve it. This will stimulate your thinking. Always aim high. The only thing that will limit your success is the thought that you can't achieve it. Be focused and when you choose something, choose it with all your might, with all your heart. Don't give up!

Work towards a timeframe. Specify a time for achieving your objectives. This is important in motivating you. To set out in the direction of your goals and keep moving towards them. Don't take your mind off your goals until you have achieved them. Be determined. Stay centered, stay positive and stay focused. Remember:

No one can stop you from reaching your GOALS. Circumstances may stop you temporarily but only YOU can stop them permanently.

🎯 Now it's time to start writing down your goals.

Write down 3 goals that you would like to achieve, and remember to be Specific.

_____
_____
_____
_____
_____
_____
_____
_____
_____
_____
_____
_____
_____
_____ Dated: __/__/__

How will you know that you are moving towards your goals? How will they be Measured?

_____
_____
_____
_____
_____
_____
_____
_____
_____
_____
_____
_____
_____ Dated: __/__/__

What can I do to ensure that my goals are Attainable?

_____
_____
_____
_____
_____
_____
_____
_____ Dated: __/__/__

What can I do to ensure that my goals remain Relevant?

_____
_____
_____
_____
_____
_____
_____
_____ Dated: __/__/__

When will my goals be achieved? How can I ensure they are being achieved within the Timeframe?

_____
_____
_____
_____
_____
_____
_____
_____
_____ Dated: __/__/__

Goals drive you to BECOME the best version of yourself.

'The real value of setting and achieving goals lies not in the rewards you receive, but in the person you become as a result of reaching your goals.'

Robin Sharma

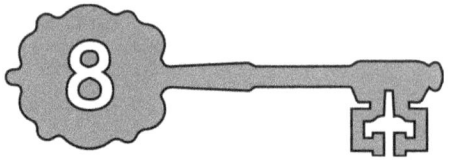

Poems, Stories and Words of Wisdom!

'Truth – living by being true, to the real you, will bring benefits you never imagined.'
Unknown

I love poems and stories, as they can lift us up, make us smile, encourage, motivate, and teach us valuable life lessons. They are like stepping stones towards living a better life. Some will make you think and some will make you cry. Hopefully, some will give you that motivation to go for your dreams.

When I was growing up, I loved storytelling. I think children have an inborn love of stories. They helped me learn and understand many wonderful things, especially how to use my imagination. Stories taught me about life, about myself and about others. Stories made things clearer in my mind. Through stories we see how very different people share the same life-experiences, and how human nature can overcome cultural barriers.

The important thing to remember when reading inspiring stories is that when you get that feeling of motivation, where you want to do something, **DO IT!** Your life will only change because of taking focused action. An inspirational story is nothing if it doesn't cause you to do something or at least make you believe in yourself a bit more. I sincerely hope you enjoy and learn from the following poems and stories. Happy reading.

Stories, The Butterfly – Giving you an empowering sense of hope

Story, Lessons from the Ant - Together everyone achieves more

Poem, Time – Time waits for no one

Poem, Who Am I? – I am habit

Poem, RUMe2? - Take control of you

Poem, One and Only You – There's only ONE of you

Words of Wisdom – Learn and practice

Story, A Message from the Geese – Stand by each other

Poem, Slow Dance – Life is not a race

Newspaper Clipping – Being responsible for your actions

Mr. Megabucks' Gateway to Wealth – Mr. Bill Gates' rules to success

Story, Perspective & Appreciation – Who is richer and who is poorer?

Poem, The Smile Starter – Smiling is contagious

I love the story of 'The Butterfly' and hopefully this will help you spark that motivational feeling, giving you an empowering sense of hope, that if they can do it, so can YOU!

 The Butterfly 'Worm Gets Ideas' (*Emmet Fox – Find and Use Your Inner Power*)

Butterflies are one of the most beautiful and interesting insects on Earth. To me, the butterfly teaches the most wonderful and the most important lesson that we human beings ever should learn. We all know the story. He is a beautiful butterfly now, but he was not always a butterfly. He began life, and he lived what seemed to him a very, very long time, as a worm – and not a very important kind of worm – what we call the humble caterpillar.

The life of a caterpillar is a sadly restricted one. He lives on a green leaf in the forest, and that is about all he knows. Then one day something happens. The little caterpillar finds certain strange stirrings going on within him. The old green leaf, for some reason, no longer seems adequate. He begins to feel dissatisfied. He becomes moody and discontented, but – it is a marvellous discontent.

He does not grumble and complain to the other caterpillars, saying 'Nature is all wrong.' 'I hate this life.' 'I can never be anything but a worm.' 'I wish that I had never been born.' He is discontented, but it is a marvellous discontent. He feels the need for a bigger, better, and more interesting life. His instinct tells him that where there is true desire there must be fulfilment, because 'where there's a will, there's a way.'

So, a wonderful thing happens. Gradually the worm disappears, and the butterfly emerges, beautiful, graceful, now endowed with wings – and instead of crawling about on a restricted leaf, he soars right above the trees, right above the forest itself – free, unrestricted, free to go where he likes, see the world, bask in the sun, and, in fact, be his own **True Self** – the free and wonderful thing that Spirit intended him to be.

Now this story is intended to be the story of every human being. It is up to you to develop your wings using your creative imagination, so that you may fly away to your heart's desire. Don't you agree?

Now let me tell you another interesting story about The Butterfly. (*Author Unknown*)

A man found a cocoon of a butterfly. One day a small opening appeared. He sat and watched the butterfly for several hours as it struggled to squeeze its body through the tiny hole. Then it stopped, as if it couldn't go further.

So, the man decided to help the butterfly. He took a pair of scissors and snipped off the remaining bits of cocoon. The butterfly emerged easily but it had a swollen body and shrivelled wings. The man continued to watch it, expecting that any minute the wings would enlarge and expand enough to support the body. Neither happened.

In fact, the butterfly spent the rest of its life crawling around. It was never able to fly.

What the man in his kindness and haste did not understand: the restricting cocoon and the struggle required by the butterfly to get through the opening was a way of forcing the fluid from the body into the wings so that it would be ready for flight once that was achieved.

Now this story tells us that sometimes struggles are exactly what we need in our lives. Going through life with no obstacles would cripple us. We will not be as strong as we could have been, and we would never fly.

"We all have struggles in our lives, but it is up to you to develop your wings by using your creative imagination and fly away to your heart's desire."

'When we are no longer able to change a situation, we are challenged to change ourselves.' **Victor Frankl**

Let's take lessons from the Ant!

(Adapted by Sompong Yusoontorn – 12 Life Lessons Ants)

Have you ever wondered about the ant how it never seems to stop moving?

Sometimes I just sit and watch them. It's intriguing when you see these tiny ants go about their business. The tiny ant can teach us great lessons. Let's see what we can learn from them.

1. Ants are well organised
There are three kinds of ants in a colony; workers, a queen and males. Each kind of ant does a different job in their community. Every day, the ant arrives at work very early and starts work immediately. They are well organised and carry out their task within their division. Nothing is left undone in the ant colony, because of the disciplined structure, which has already been put into place.

This is a serious lesson for individuals who are not organised.

2. Unselfishness within the colony
There is no 'I' in Ant. For ants, it is simple: do your job and do it right and all the ants in the colony will benefit from it. Ants have an unbelievable spirit of unselfishness. If they find something edible, immediately they pass on the message to others. They eat what they need today. They eat enough to get them through the winter.

All for one and one for all!

3. Spirit of sharing
The Ants share everything they find. They never eat anything alone. They show great interest in sharing. But what do we humans do? We often fill our plates, don't like to share, and sometimes we don't even finish! At times humans can be greedy and wasteful.

Only a few have experienced the taste and pleasure of sharing. Sharing is caring.

4. Amazing sense of discipline
The sense of discipline among the ants is amazing. Without a mistake, they march one after the other in a line. Have you ever witnessed them marching? What a sight to behold! Without any dispute or accident, they move about in order.

Discipline is doing what you don't want to do when you don't want to do it.

5. Action in time
The ant has no master or overseer. The ant secures food in summer and stores up provisions during harvest time.

This is a reminder to humans to be alert and active.

6. Ants are tireless
Ants always keep themselves busy all day long. They are busy doing something, unlike many individuals who are busy doing nothing. Like Henry David Thoreau said, 'It is not enough to be busy, so are the ants. The question is: What are we busy about?'

To be tireless means never slacking or stopping until the work is done.

7. Ants are persistent
Ants are persistent. Whenever an obstacle is placed in the way of Ants, they always find a way around that obstacle. Napoleon said, 'Victory belongs to the persistent.' We must never give up so easily in the face of obstacles. There are many obstacles in life that must be overcome.

If you keep trying you will get past whatever is blocking your path.

8. Ants have Incredible Speed
Ants may be small in nature, but never underrate their speed.

This is a big lesson for those who are sluggish in doing things or making decisions.

9. Ants are great Planners
Ants know that summer – the good times – won't last forever. Ants think about winter all summer. When it is winter, they store up enough food in their colony. As during winter, when the cold becomes unbearable, they never lack anything.

Ants are better planners than some individuals. Winters will come. Plan.

10. Ants are strong and hardworking
Ants are noted for carrying objects that are bigger than them. This is only made possible through sheer hard work and determination. Ants are not only strong, but they are hard working. They are not scared of heavy tasks, but rather take pleasure in carrying objects to their colony.

If you are walking up a mountain, don't focus on the top of the mountain but focus on each individual step you take.

11. Ants practice teamwork
Everything an ant does is for the benefit of the colony and they will work until they are done. Each ant knows its duties and does everything it can to get those duties completed. Some are tunnelling, some are moving material and others are looking for food. If any ant is not working with the team, they will be noticed.

Together **E**veryone **A**chieves **M**ore

12. Ants make the most of every opportunity
Ants are surprisingly smart – you see what makes ants so smart is that they think together. If they are headed somewhere and you try to stop them, they will look for another way.

The problem is, many people are easily distracted on the way to their opportunities.

'Watching ants at work and play is amazing. The lessons from these tiny ants are great challenges for mankind. The lessons they teach will lead us to an insightful life and success.'

Another Great Poem – Time!

Value each moment as this poem so strikingly states.

Imagine there is a bank which credits your account each morning with **$86,400**. It carries over no balance from day to day. Every evening it deletes whatever part of the balance you failed to use during the day. What would you do? Draw out every cent each day, of course!

We all have such a bank account and its name is called **TIME**. Every morning it credits you with **86,400 Seconds**. Every night, it writes off, as lost, whatever amount you have failed to put to good use. Each night, it burns the remainders of the day. If you failed to use the day's deposits, the loss is yours. There is no drawing against the 'tomorrow.'

You must **live in the present**, on today's deposits. Invest it to get from it the ultimate in health, happiness and success. The clock is running – make the most of today. Because:

If you think **One Year** is not important,
Ask the student who repeated a year.
If you think **One Month** is not important,
Ask a mother who gave birth to a premature baby.
If you think **One Week** is not important,
Ask an editor of a weekly magazine.
If you think **One Hour** is not important,
Ask the lovers who are waiting to meet.
If you think **One Minute** is not important,
Ask a person who missed their train.
If you think **One Second** is not important,
Ask the person who just avoided an accident.
If you think **One Millisecond** is not important,
Ask the person who won a silver medal in the Olympics instead of gold.

Treasure every moment you have and treasure it more because you shared it with someone special - special enough to spend your time on.

REMEMBER THAT TIME WAITS FOR NO ONE

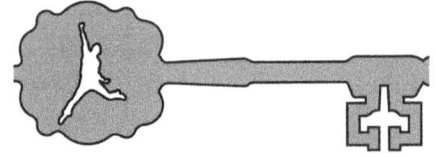

This poem is so relevant: Right Here, Right Now!

Who Am I?
(Author Unknown)

I am your constant companion.

I am your greatest helper or heaviest burden.

I will push you onward or drag you down to failure.

I am completely at your command.

Half of the things you do you might as well turn over to me and I will do them - quickly and correctly.

I am easily managed - you must be firm with me.

Show me exactly how you want something done and after a few lessons, I will do it automatically.

I am the servant of great people, and alas, of all failures as well.

Those who are great, I have made great.

Those who are failures, I have made failures.

I am not a machine though I work with the precision of a machine plus the intelligence of a person.

You may run me for profit or run me for ruin - it makes no difference to me.

Take me, train me, be firm with me, and I will place the world at your feet.

Be easy with me and I will destroy you.

I am Habit!

Remember, our thoughts create our habits. Thoughts.

RUMe2 (Are You Me Too)!
(Denis Waitley, The Psychology of Winning)

Each of us has our own 'self-image robot' in our mind named RUMe2 (sub-conscience mind). 'I am the voice inside you who tells you whether or not you really can do something.' A poem to illustrate the point:

My Robot (Self-Image)

I have a little Robot
That goes around with me;
I tell him what I'm thinking.
I tell him what I see.
I tell my little Robot
All my hopes and fears;
He listens and remembers
All my joys and tears!
At first my little ROBOT
Followed my command;
But after years of training
He's gotten out of hand.
He doesn't care what's right or wrong
Or what is false or true;
No matter what I try – now;
He tells me what to do!

During every moment of our lives we program our 'self-image robot' to work for us, or against us. It's only function is to follow our previous instructions, unnoticeably, just like a personal computer playing back what is stored – responding automatically. Much of the information fed into our 'self-image robot's' memory stays there.

I sincerely hope this poem makes you think twice about your thoughts. Start taking control of YOU, the inner YOU! You owe it to yourself.

One and Only You!
(James T. Moore)

Every single blade of grass,
And every flake of snow –
Is just a wee bit different...
There's no two alike, you know.

From something small, like grains of sand,
To each gigantic star
All were made with THIS in mind:
To be just what they are!

How foolish then, to imitate –
How useless to pretend!
Since each of us comes from a MIND
Whose ideas never end.

There'll only be just ONE of ME
To show what I can do –
And you should likewise feel very proud,
There's only ONE of YOU.

That is where it all starts
With you, a wonderful
Unlimited human being!

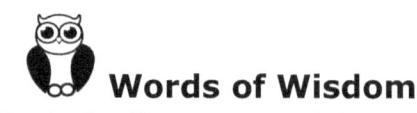
Words of Wisdom
(Paulo Coelho, Warrior of the Light)

'If someone comes to you with a gift and you do not accept it, who does the gift belong to?' asked the samurai.

'To the person who tried to deliver it,' replied one of the disciples.

'The same goes for envy, anger and insults,' said the master. 'When they are not accepted, they continue to belong to those who carried them.'

All it takes is 90 Seconds
(Jim Fannin)

Wow, I just finished reading an article by Jim Fannin; I was so impressed I had to share it with you.

If you haven't seen someone for a while, say even two hours (family members) make sure you greet them by giving them 90 seconds of your **full attention**.

You see, the first 90 seconds that you see a person has more impact on the relationship than you spending hours and hours with them later.

Make sure in that first 90 seconds you make eye contact. That way you can tell what kind of day they are having and respond appropriately.

That's the deal.

It's amazing how it makes you feel and the person you have greeted as well.

We are always in a hurry and unintentionally greet people by just saying,

'Hi, how are you?' and never really listening to their reply.

Let's turn the key to change by giving 90 seconds of your enthusiastic attention to EVERYONE.

Physical Goals
(Unknown)

Too many people confine their exercise to:
Running up bills
Stretching the truth
Bending over backwards
Lying down on the job
Side-stepping responsibility and
Pushing their luck! But not **YOU!**

Hugging
(Unknown)

Did you know that **HUGGING** is healthy?
It helps the immune system, cures depression,
reduces stress and induces sleep.
It's invigorating.
It's rejuvenating and has no unpleasant side effects.

It's natural.
It has no artificial ingredients, as it's organic,
naturally sweet, non-polluting, environmentally friendly
and 100% wholesome.

Think of people in your life who need a **HUG**.
Are there any **HUGS** you want to share?
What are you waiting for?
Hoping someone else will ask first?
Please don't wait. Initiate!

A Message from the Geese
(Unknown)

Did you know that Geese fly along in a 'V' formation? You might be interested to learn what researchers have discovered about why they fly that way.

It has been learnt that as each bird flaps its wings, it creates an uplift for the bird immediately following. By flying in a 'V' formation, the whole flock adds at least 71% greater flying range than if each bird flew on its own.

People who share a common direction and sense of community can get where they are going quicker and easier, because they are travelling on the thrust of one another.

When a goose falls out of formation, it suddenly feels the drag and resistance of trying to go it alone, and quickly gets back into formation to take advantage of the lifting power of the bird immediately in front.

If we had as much sense as a goose, we would stay in formation with those who are heading in the same direction we are going. When the lead goose gets tired, he rotates back in the wing and another goose files 'point'. It pays to take turns doing hard jobs – with people or with geese flying.

The geese honk from behind to encourage those up front, to keep up their speed. What messages do we give when we honk from behind?

Finally, when a goose gets sick, or is wounded by gunshot and falls out of formation, two geese follow to protect and help him. They stay with him until he is either able to fly or until he dies, and then they launch out on their own or with another formation to catch up with their group again.

If we had the sense of a goose and practiced it, we would stand by each other like they do. **Safety in numbers.**

Slow Dance
(David L. Weatherford)

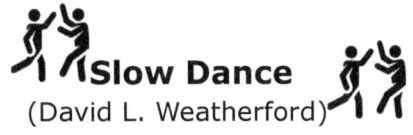

Life Is Not A Race.

Have you ever watched kids on a merry-go-round,
or listened to rain slapping the ground?

Ever followed a butterfly's erratic flight,
or gazed at the sun fading into the night?

You better slow down, don't dance so fast,
time is short, the music won't last.

Do you run through each day on the fly,
when you ask 'How are you?' do you hear the reply?

When the day is done, do you lie in your bed,
with the next hundred chores running through your head?

You better slow down, don't dance so fast,
time is short, the music won't last.

Ever told your child, we'll do it tomorrow,
and in your haste, not see his sorrow?

Ever lost touch, let a friendship die,
because you never had time to call and say hi?

You better slow down, don't dance so fast,
time is short, the music won't last.

When you run so fast to get somewhere,
you miss half the fun of getting there.

When you worry and hurry through your day,
it's like an unopened gift thrown away.

Life isn't a race, so take it slower,
and hear the music before your song is over.

NEWS

Just recently I was handed a newspaper clipping and I thought you might benefit from it. I had a laugh when I read it and thought this Judge was very wise indeed. See what you think?

Here's an excerpt from an open letter to teenagers that came from a Judge at a Brisbane Juvenile Court.

Always, we hear the cry from teenagers, 'What can we do? Where can we go? I'm bored.'

His answer:

> Go home, mow the lawn, wash the windows, learn to cook, build a raft, get a job, visit the sick, study your lessons, and after you have finished, read a book!
> Your town does not owe you recreation facilities.
> Your parents do not owe you fun.
> The world does not owe you a living.
>
> You owe the world something.
> You owe it your **time, energy and talents**, so that no one will be at war, in poverty or sick and lonely again.
> In other words, grow up, stop being a cry-baby, get out of your dream world and develop a backbone, not a wishbone.
>
> Start behaving like a responsible person.
> You are important and you are needed.
> It's too late to sit around and wait for somebody to do something someday.
> Someday is now and that somebody is **YOU!**

**Powerful, Right? Be true to yourself.
Believe in something, you will achieve.
Destiny is in your hands.**

💲 Mr. Megabucks' Gateway to Wealth 💲

Mr. Bill Gates – Microsoft – Originally Published in the *San Diego Union-Tribune* in September 1996.

Rule 1	Life is not fair ... Get used to it!
Rule 2	The world will not care about your self-esteem. The world will expect you to accomplish something before you feel good about yourself.
Rule 3	You will not make $60,000 a year straight out of high school. You will not be a Vice-President with a car phone until you earn both.
Rule 4	If you think your teacher is tough, wait until you get a boss.
Rule 5	Flipping burgers is not beneath your dignity. Your grandparents had a different word for burger flipping – they called it opportunity.
Rule 6	If you mess up, it is not your parents' fault, so do not whine about your mistakes, learn from them.
Rule 7	Before you were born, your parents were not as boring as they are now. They became that way from paying your bills, cleaning your clothes and listening to you talk about how cool you thought you were. So, before you save the rainforest from the parasites of your parents' generation, try delousing the closet in your own room.
Rule 8	Your school may have done away with winners and losers, but life has not. In some schools, they have abolished failing grades and they will give you as many times as you want to get the right answer. This does not bear the slightest resemblance to anything in real life.
Rule 9	Life is not divided into semesters. You do not get summers off and few employers are interested in helping you find yourself. Do that on your own time.
Rule 10	Television is not real life. In real life, people actually have to leave the coffee shop and go to jobs.
Rule 11	Be nice to nerds. Chances are you will end up working for one.

An Interesting Story on Perspective and Appreciation

Who Is Richer and Who Is Poorer?

One day a father of a very wealthy family took his son on a trip to the country with the purpose of showing him how poor people live. They spent a couple of days and nights on a farm of what would be considered a very poor family.

On their return from their trip, the father asked his son; 'How was the trip?' 'It was great Dad,' said the boy. 'Did you see how poor people live?' the father asked. 'Oh yeah,' said the son. 'So, tell me what you learned from the trip?' asked the father.

> The son answered: 'I saw that we have one dog and they had four.
> We have a pool that reaches to the middle of our garden and they have a creek that has no end.
>
> We have imported lanterns in our garden and they have the stars at night.
> Our patio reaches to the front yard and they have the whole horizon. We have a small piece of land to live on and they have fields that go beyond.
>
> We have servants who serve us, but they serve others. We buy our food, but they grow theirs. We have walls around our property to protect us, they have friends to protect them.'

The boy's father was speechless. Then his son added, 'Thanks dad for showing me how poor we are.'

**Interesting... makes you put things into perspective.
Don't take things for granted.
Don't worry about what you don't have.
Appreciate what you do have!**

*'Be happy in the moment, that's enough.
Each moment is all we need, not more.'*
Mother Teresa

The Smile Starter

Smiling is contagious
and you can catch it like the flu.
When someone smiled at me today,
I started smiling too.

I passed around the corner,
and someone saw my grin.
When he smiled - I realised,
I'd passed it onto him.

I thought about that smile,
then I realised its worth.
A single smile just like mine,
could travel around the Earth.

So, if you feel a smile begin,
please don't leave it undetected.
Let's start an epidemic,
and get the world infected!

Remember, that the brain doesn't know the difference between a real smile and a pretend smile. Pretend to smile whenever you feel down and out. Then, guess what? It will bring you that positive feeling.

And the best thing is: a smile is FREE!

Remember my Vitamin D for Determination? To
focus on my purpose of making a difference to whomever I meet, whether it is with words of encouragement, a hug or just a warm friendly smile.

Let me share this crazy idea with you, something you can do whenever life seems tough or you are just having one of those days... It's quite simple. Go grab a pen.

Hold up your index finger and draw a ☺ ... now wriggle your finger!

I know you will start laughing, it's so weird, but it works!

This is something you can use at school, the office, at home or socially to lighten the mood.

A smile is a curved line that sets things straight.

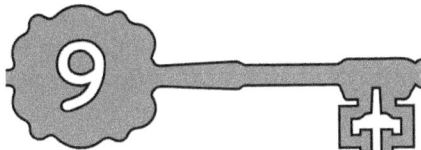

It's Your Time to Unlock Your Mind!

'The only limits we have are the limits we believe.'
Wayne Dyer

I dedicated this book to YOU, **The Incredible Awesome YOU!** Together, we took a stand for change. I have a passion and burning desire to encourage and motivate people to reach their potential, turning it into active energy, igniting the flame within. I believe that our background and circumstances may have influenced who we are today, but we are responsible for who we become. We are always growing. Together we can make a difference and leave our legacy behind.

It's been a real honour to guide you towards reaching your true potential to live an amazing life. A life you deserve. You were born with a greatness to be the TRUE you and your best can still be in front of you. Everything takes time. Can you imagine getting to the end of your life just to discover that you wasted it? You are the author of your life!

Now is the time to step up and be counted. **You are unique!** The alternative is, of course, to say; 'That was a great read, a very interesting book, full of info,' then put the book on a shelf and carry on with your old habits. Gosh, that would be sad, only because nothing much in your life will change. If you took the time to read **'The Incredible Awesome YOU'** you clearly want to improve some things in your life, right? All I ask of YOU is to have a go.

Yes, it will take time but with a little patience, practice and persistence, new habits will become a part of who you aspire to be. Go for something you want so badly, that you think about it all the time. Your approach should be from **NO-WHERE** to **NOW-HERE**. Then a year from now you'll be saying, 'Look how much I've changed, and look at my results – I can hardly believe it.' Then, celebrate your magnificence.

Decide, right now, to refocus and become **"The Incredible Awesome You!"** Why not consider pulling the book back off the shelf every six months, to assess your goals and evaluate your growth. Let this stir you up to achieve even more, to keep heading in the direction of your true purpose in life. Do all you can and more – all that you possibly can to make it happen.

Remember. You have nothing to deal with, but your own thoughts.

Remember. Your life is what your thoughts make it.

Remember. *Words* are so powerful that one word can transform or destroy a life.

Remember. Life is for laughing, loving and living, not for whining, worrying and wasting.

Remember. To inject yourself with the Daily Mental Vitamins and have a terrific day today, tomorrow and every day for the rest of your life.

Attitude, **B**elief, **C**ourage, **D**etermination, **E**nthusiasm, **F**orgiveness and **G**ratitude

Be all that you can be. How will you ever know your true potential in life, unless you keep reaching, stretching and pushing beyond your limits? So, may I suggest, just push, press and stretch yourself, and keep doing it until you become larger than life. You Can Do It! **Attitude is the magic word.**

Some words of encouragement. Do not be afraid. Fight those feelings with all your strength; it is vital that you do this, if you are to reach your true potential. Don't let your fear of past events affect the outcome of your future. *Live for what today must offer,* not what yesterday has taken away. What we see depends on how we look at it. Forget what you've lost and focus on what you've learnt. You are now on your way to a future with a purpose.

Think positive. Say positive things to yourself. Focus on what is developing today and the good things that might happen. Always seek ways to improve yourself. **You are unique!** Never ever forget that. There is no one like you and there never will be.

Let's face it; it's not always easy to ask for help, so

- To apologise – **Say sorry.**
- To begin over – **Tomorrow is a new day.**
- To be unselfish – **Do something for someone else.**
- To take advice – **Ask for help.**
- To admit to an error – **I was wrong.**
- To keep trying – **Soldier on.**
- To be considerate – **Think of others.**
- To avoid mistakes – **Think twice.**
- To forgive and forget – **Be humble.**
- To think and then act – **Act.**
- To make the best of a little – **It's the little things that make a difference.**

Some words from me to YOU:

Like a butterfly, it is time for us to spread our wings
You in one direction and me in the other
But whether together or apart
Let's fly towards our destination and create the magic
We were destined to share!

More About the Author.
Who Is Angelika Jankovic?

*'Don't be afraid to learn.
Knowledge is weightless, a treasure you can always carry easily.'*
Author Unknown

I have a passion and a burning desire to encourage and motivate people to reach their potential, turning it into active energy, igniting the flame within. Sometimes their potential is hidden, but sooner or later, they discover it and head in the direction of their true purpose in life. Therefore, making a difference within their circle of influence or even the world.

Over the years, I've learnt how important it is to be aware of our thoughts. No one ever tells us that our thoughts dictate our future. Our thoughts make us who we are today. Think about it. Thoughts become actions. If we think happy thoughts, we will be happy. If we think negative thoughts, we will be negative. If we think failure, we will certainly fail. If we act energetically, we become energetic. You can control what you think. But, nobody ever tells us that.

My purpose in writing **The Incredible Awesome YOU** is to help you understand how important your attitude is towards yourself and others, this will make such a difference to your life. You and I are responsible for our lives. Everything we say or do will cause a domino effect. You and I produce causes all day long, every day of our lives. The environment can only return to us what we give out. Therefore, I say that each of us determines the quality of our lives. We get back what we put out.

Here is a way to evaluate the quality of your attitude in the past. Would you say people tend to react to you in a smiling, positive manner, giving you friendly greetings when you appear? Your answer to that question will tell the story. Nothing can change until **YOU** do. When **YOU** change, your world will change. The answer is **Attitude!**

***A small spark can start a great fire.
Continue your journey towards a healthy attitude keeping the flame burning!***

***Your future will be bright,
if your attitude is right!***

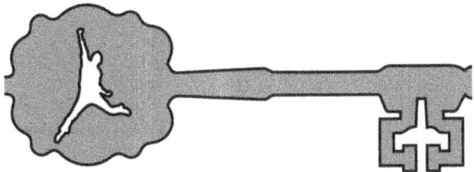

***Your future will be bright,
if your attitude is right!***

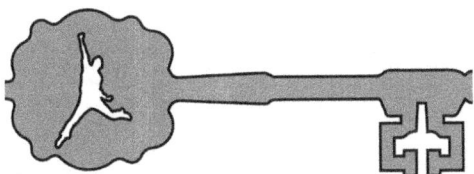

www.ingramcontent.com/pod-product-compliance
Lightning Source LLC
Chambersburg PA
CBHW072056290426
44110CB00014B/1699